Also by J. I. Merritt

Trout Dreams

Goodbye, Liberty Belle

Baronets and Buffalo

The Best of Field & Stream (ed.)

The Derrydale Press Treasury of Fishing (ed.)

THE LAST BUFFALO HUNT
AND OTHER STORIES

THE LAST BUFFALO HUNT AND OTHER STORIES

ADVENTURES IN THE GREAT AMERICAN OUTDOORS

J.I. Merritt

Illustrations by the author

South River Press
Pennington, New Jersey

ISBN 10: 1-59152-105-X
ISBN 13: 978-1-59152-105-1

South River Press / J.I. Merritt

The pieces in this anthology originally appeared in different form in *Field & Stream* and other publications. For details, see pages 185-194.

J.I. Merritt / South River Press, 51 N. Main St., Pennington, NJ 08534; www.southriverpress.com; southriverpress@gmail.com.

This book can be ordered from Farcountry Press (800-821-3874; www.farcountrypress.com).

Printed and distributed by Sweetgrass Books; P.O. Box 5630, Helena, MT 59604; 800-821-3874; www.sweetgrassbooks.com.

Printed in the United States.

15 14 13 12 1 2 3 4 5 6 7

For George Reiger and Lamar Underwood

Contents

THE LAST BUFFALO HUNT
AND OTHER STORIES

1

The Long Hunter: Daniel Boone

In the spring of 1769, six men rode west from the upper Yadkin Valley in North Carolina, bound for a country beyond the mountains they called *Kan-ta-ke*, an Indian name meaning meadows or fields. They wore wide-brimmed felt hats that shaded their chiseled features, long homespun hunting shirts belted at the waist, buckskin leggings over linen breeches, and moccasins. Each man cradled that peerless weapon of the American frontier, a Pennsylvania long rifle. A powder horn and bullet pouch hung from his shoulder, and a sheathed hunting knife and a tomahawk were tucked in his belt. Pack horses trailing behind carried traps, camp kettles, smithing tools, and extra rifles, powder, shot, and flints.

They expected to be gone at least six months, and their leader, a thirty-four-year-old backwoodsman whose wilderness exploits were already the stuff of legend, expected to be gone a spell longer than that. It would be two years before Daniel Boone again laid eyes on the Yadkin Valley and the cabin that was home to him and his wife, Rebecca, and their six children. Rebecca was pregnant with their seventh child, but she had long ago resigned herself to her husband's absences. For Boone was a "long hunter," one of a breed of frontiersman who routinely left his family for months at a stretch to harvest skins and pelts for the market. Most long hunters confined their absences to the fall and winter, leaving home after the crops were in and returning in time for the spring planting. But the community granted Boone and a few others tacit exemption from such obligations, especially once sons were old enough for field work, and Daniel's eldest boys were now twelve and ten.

This was neither Boone's first long hunt nor his last — he had been a professional hunter since age sixteen, and to his family's consternation he would continue to make lengthy trips afield well into his seventies. It would, however, be his first venture into the fabled hunting grounds beyond the Appalachians. Kentucky was a vast Indian game preserve shared by the Cherokees to the south and the Shawnees inhabiting villages north of it on the Ohio River. The Indians hunted in Kentucky and passed through it, but did not live there. Nor, for a while longer at least, did whites.

Riding with Boone as they crossed into present-day eastern Tennessee and through a cut in the mountains called the Cumberland Gap were his brother-in-law John Stewart, a frontier trader named John Findley, and three others. Boone had known Findley since 1755, when they had served together in the French and Indian War. Three years before they met, Findley had penetrated Kentucky's interior from the Ohio River, and he filled the young backwoodsman's head with visions of a country teeming with deer, elk, bear, turkey, and woodland buffalo.

Findley's tales pulled at Boone. Later, when the trader showed up in the Yadkin settlements and the two men renewed their friendship, the talk turned inevitably to this land of near-mythic bounty. Findley thought he knew a way of getting to Kentucky directly from these mountains, and the long hunt they were embarked on now was a test of that notion. At the Cumberland Gap they picked up a trail known to the Cherokees as the Warrior's Path and followed it north.

FIVE WEEKS AFTER LEAVING the Upper Yadkin, Boone climbed a hill called Pilot Knob and surveyed an endless rolling landscape. Stretched before him was a country that came up to Findley's brag and then some. The hardwood forests and dense canebrakes

Daniel Boone retained the archetypal features of a backwoodsman until the end of his long life. This drawing of him is based on a portrait painted in 1820, when he was 83.

were laced with buffalo trails, or "traces" — wide swaths that would later serve as pioneer roads. The traces led to "licks" bubbling with mineral springs that drew buffalo by the thousands. In other places the forest opened up to bluegrass meadows grazed by herds of elk and deer. Equating the absence of trees with poor soil, early settlers referred to these woodland glades as "barrens." In fact, central Kentucky's limestone substrate made for a fertile soil, and the Indians' custom of seasonally firing the glades further enhanced their productivity. (The burning killed tree seedlings and promoted a varied habitat that supported more game.) Surprisingly, bluegrass was not a native species but timothy, an English import that had spread inland earlier in the century, its seeds borne in the packing straw of Ohio River traders.

The party set up base camp — a simple lean-to, fire pit, and scaffolding to keep dressed hides and meat away from predators — and fell into a routine that would carry them through the summer and fall. Usually two men remained in camp dressing skins and jerking meat while the others paired off and went looking for game. Boone and Stewart generally worked together and might stay out for a week or more. Mainly they hunted deer. On the market, a dressed buckskin would fetch the equivalent of a German silver coin called a *thaler* (eventually, "buck" became synonymous with "dollar"). Less valuable elk skins were cut into "tugs" or ropes for use in camp, and the undressed hides of bear and buffalo were used for bedding and to wrap the bales of dressed deer skins. In winter, when beaver pelts were prime, they switched to trapping.

Boone and his five companions were the first long hunters to arrive in Kentucky via the Cumberland Gap, but others soon followed. That same summer of 1769, Boone's friend Caspar Mansker took a party of twenty through the Gap and hunted along the future border of Kentucky and Tennessee, and the following fall, fifty men entered the bluegrass country led by two other long hunters of renown, Joseph Drake and Henry Skaggs.

Skaggs, described by one early chronicler as a "bold, enterprising, and fearless" man of "large and bony frame," was Scots-Irish, the grandson of immigrants from Protestant Northern Ireland. His ancestry was typical of most long hunters and the people of Appalachia generally. As a group the Scots-Irish were tough, flinty, clannish, independent, and hostile to authority. To a greater or lesser degree such qualities were shared by all who embraced the communal isolation of mountain life, whatever their family's country of origin, which in the Yadkin settlements also included England and Germany.

Boone's forebears were English and Welsh Quakers who first settled near Reading, Pennsylvania, where Daniel was born in 1734. The rambunctious fourth boy and sixth child (of eleven) of Squire and Sarah Boone could run like a deer and swim like an otter. As a child tending the family cows he sharpened the end of his herdsman's staff and used it to spear small game. By age thirteen he was ranging farther afield, hunting opossums and raccoons with his first gun, a smoothbore. By the time his family moved on to Virginia and then to North Carolina, he had acquired his first rifle. He was soon winning shooting matches against men twice his age, even — as a self-imposed handicap — when firing from a one-armed stance.

Boone was blessed with keen intelligence, exceptional eyesight and reflexes, and the instincts of a born hunter, but as a boy he picked up most of his basic knowledge about tracking, stalking, and decoying from the Delaware and Shawnee Indians who gathered at his grandfather's mill. This was not unusual, for few New World immigrants arrived knowing anything about hunting, an activity that Old World laws restricted to landed gentry. It was Native Americans who taught European Americans how to hunt. The Indian tactics adopted by whites varied according to game, conditions, and personal preference. Frontiersmen were subsistence hunters, with no concept of conservation, and by today's standards some of their methods would be flat-out illegal, not to mention unethical. Some of the most popular and effective ways involved fire. These included jacklighting — using a torch to find and freeze deer at night — and encircling deer in a ring of flames and shooting them as they bolted in panic. Boone did some "fire hunting" as a boy but disapproved of it as a man. It was too easy and required a companion. He preferred hunting alone and in a manner that challenged his woodcraft. He liked hunting from a stand and, better yet, "still" hunting — following sign in a slow upwind stalk that might take hours to put him in shooting range of his quarry.

He was also adept at "barking off" a squirrel: hitting a spot on a branch just below a squirrel's perch. The shock of the bullet's impact killed the squirrel indirectly, sparing the meat.

Like their native counterparts, white males in mountain settlements did most of their hunting in the hours around dawn and dusk and at the rising of the moon, when game was most likely up and about. Depending on inclination, during the day they might or might not put in much time behind a plow, often leaving such field work to women and children. Long hunters like

Elisha Walden, who bragged that he had "never cultivated the soil," were even less inclined toward farming. Henry Skaggs was reputedly so ignorant of farm chores that he did not even know how bacon was cured, and Boone — described by a nephew as "ever impractical of the business of farming" — gave it up at the earliest opportunity. This apparent bias against honest work appalled colonial gentry and clergy, who concluded that hunting debased whites by making them like Indians. Backwoods hunters, sniffed one observer, were a "people of abandon'd Morals and profligate Principles, the lowest Pack of Wretches my eyes ever saw." Another was shocked to see how "they delight in their present low, lazy, sluttish, heathenish, hellish Life, and seem not desirous of changing it."

Such critics, of course, overlooked the long hunter's ability to survive by his wits in a wilderness where injury and hostile Indians were constant threats. Nor did they acknowledge his self-sufficiency and sheer practical know-how. A long hunter made his own clothes and accouterments and repaired his rifle with parts he forged himself. He cast his own bullets and mixed his own black powder, a concoction of 10 parts sulfur, 15 parts charcoal, and 75 parts saltpeter leached from outhouse nightsoil or bat guano dug from caves. The long hunter's understanding of the animals he hunted and the wild plants he foraged for food and medicine surpassed that of any Latin-spouting naturalist and enabled him to live more or less indefinitely off the land.

Seven months into Boone's long hunt in Kentucky, Shawnees got the drop on his party and relieved it of a season's worth of deer skins. Every long hunter lived with this risk; Henry Skaggs once returned to camp to find that Indians had scattered his pelts and hides on the ground and left them to rot — "1500 skins gone to ruination." From the Indians' point of view the whites were poachers and their goods contraband. The Shawnees might have killed Boone and his companions on the spot, but their leader let them go with a warning: Come here again, he said, and "you may be sure the wasps and yellow-jackets will sting you severely."

The Shawnees also took their horses and long rifles but left them with some cheap trade guns and enough powder and shot to make it back to the settlements. But Boone wasn't done with Kentucky. On the homeward trek, the six hunters encountered Daniel's younger brother Squire coming into the country with a fresh load of supplies. While Findley and two others stuck to their decision to return home, the Boone brothers, along with John Stewart and a fourth man, headed back down the Warrior's Path.

Late that winter, Stewart left camp to check his traplines and was never seen alive again. Five years later, when Boone returned to the area at the head of a party cutting the Wilderness Road to open Kentucky to settlement, by chance someone found in the hollow of a sycamore tree a skeleton and a powder horn that Boone recognized as Stewart's. He surmised that Indians had chanced upon his brother-in-law while tending his traps and shot him. Stewart managed to escape his pursuers and take shelter in the tree, then died from his wounds.

Boone brooded over his kin's fate, but in a grimly literal sense violent death went with the long hunter's territory. It would not be the last time one of Boone's loved ones died at the hands of Indians. Three year's after Stewart's disappearance, a Cherokee tortured and killed Boone's eldest child, sixteen-year-old James, and left his body riddled with arrows. The fighting between Indians and whites during the bloody settling of Kentucky also cost him another son, a brother, and a nephew — and years later, during the settling of Missouri, a grandson. Until the end of his days Boone couldn't talk about these losses without breaking into tears, yet it is a testament to his Quaker temperament that he never became an Indian hater. Perhaps at some level he realized that whites were the true aggressors.

Following Stewart's death, Boone spent another fourteen months in Kentucky. Brother Squire made several trips between their base camp and the Yadkin, bringing out skins and returning with supplies. The younger Boone was astonished at Daniel's ability to endure hardship — the meaner conditions got, the more he seemed to thrive. Once, during a driving rainstorm, they took refuge under a horse blanket. Squire was wet, cold, and hungry and told Daniel he'd had it with the wilderness, but "I believe you would be satisfied to remain here forever." Replied Daniel, "You would do better not to fret about it, but try to content yourself with what we cannot help."

For one three-month stretch Boone was alone except for the companionship of three dogs and his two favorite books, the Bible and *Gulliver's Travels.* (Kentucky's Lulbegrud Creek, named by Boone, is a corruption of a place name in Swift's satire.) If he sensed the presence of Indians he kept a cold camp or slept in caves. At other times he scarcely bothered to hide his presence, singing and talking aloud by a blazing fire.

ACCOMPANIED BY SQUIRE, Daniel in the spring of 1771 finally returned to North Carolina. According to family lore, his reunion with Rebecca took place at a hoe-down. Boone's hair and beard had grown long during his two years in Kentucky and he had the look of a wild man — so changed in appearance that at first his wife didn't recognize him and spurned his request for a dance. The scales fell from her eyes when the grizzled stranger replied with a laugh, "You need not refuse, for you have danced many a time with me." The Yadkin Valley's Odysseus and his Penelope locked in joyous embrace. As related by a Boone descendant, for the rest of the evening the long hunter regaled the crowd with "the story of his hardships and adventures in the romantic land of Kentucky, where he had encountered bears, Indians, and wild cats — and had seen a country wonderful in its beauty to behold."

A counterpoint to this lovely tale — in its own way just as affecting — is the story of another Boone reunion. A decade earlier, Daniel had returned from a militia campaign against the Cherokees in eastern Tennessee. He had been gone the better part of two years, long enough for Rebecca to fear he'd been killed. When he arrived home he found his wife cradling a month-old baby girl. A weeping Rebecca confessed: assuming he was dead, she had taken up briefly with his younger brother Ned. (According to a family friend, the Boone boys looked so much alike that Rebecca "couldn't help it.") Nonplussed at first by this startling news, Daniel quickly adjusted. Shaking it off, he replied, "So much the better, it's all in the family."

HOWEVER JOYFUL his return, Boone had little to show for his two years' absence. On the homeward journey Indians had stolen his entire winter's take of beaver pelts. It was a devastating loss, at least as bad as the earlier theft of deer skins. Characteristically, he took the calamity in stride, for the knowledge he'd gained about Kentucky was worth a fortune in hides. Four years later, in 1775, he led the first pioneers through the Cumberland Gap, and wave upon wave soon followed. Joining the great migration he'd started, in 1779 Boone and his family rode west to resettle in the glady bluegrass country.

Over the next decade, as more settlers poured into Kentucky, Boone fought Indians and continued to market hunt, in one three-week stretch killing 155 bears. (There was a ready market for bear pelts and the grease rendered from their flesh.) In 1791, the year before Kentucky separated from Virginia, he briefly served as a representative in the state assembly.

He also tried his hand as a tavern keeper, surveyor, and land agent, but he turned out to be even worse at business than he'd been at farming. Creditors sued him, and the state confiscated land he owned for failure to pay taxes.

For Boone, Kentucky was proving to be less than the Promised Land. It was filling up, at least by his standards, and its game mostly gone — in no small measure due to market hunters like himself. Like Hawkeye, the character in James Fenimore Cooper's Leatherstocking Tales who was modeled on Boone, he felt a deep ambivalence about his role in westward expansion and what "comes of settling a country." It was time to move on.

So in 1799, at age sixty-four, he packed all his earthly goods in a dugout canoe and with Rebecca headed down the Ohio for Missouri. With most of the Boones' seven surviving children and their families, they settled on a bluff overlooking the Missouri River, well beyond other settlements. Boone turned seventy in 1804 but still had the itch. He hunted and trapped along the Missouri and its tributaries, usually alone or with a black man named Derry Coburn. A slave owned by his son Daniel Morgan Boone, Derry became his closest companion.

In 1810, when Boone was seventy-five, two friends from his Kentucky days dropped by on their way up the Missouri. Boone and Derry joined them. They may have reached the Yellowstone River in present-day Montana. After six months, Boone returned with sixty beaver skins. It was his last long hunt.

When Rebecca died two years later, Boone had a coffin of black walnut made for her and an identical one for himself. Sometimes he took naps in it and enjoyed the bemusement this caused. Rheumatism wracked his now-frail frame, and his eyes were failing although not his spirit. At age eighty-three he went on a brief hunt with his seventeen-year-old grandson, James, but packed it in after two days because of cold. On September 26, 1820, two months short of his eighty-sixth birthday, he died in the home of a daughter, surrounded by three generations of Boones. "My time has come," he said.

The long hunter was gone, but his spirit endures. The poet Stephen Vincent Benét imagined him on cold fall evenings, gliding through the forest under a rising moon:

When Daniel Boone goes by, at night
the phantom deer arise
And all lost, wild America
Is burning in their eyes.

2

William Bartram in America's Eden

On a gentle May afternoon in 1775, halfway through his four-year-long exploration of the American Southeast, William Bartram stood on a ridge in the Nantahala Mountains of North Carolina and gazed into an enchanted valley. Bartram recorded the scene later in his famous *Travels*: deer grazed in the spring meadow and wild turkeys strutted among the wildflowers while a company of Indian girls cavorted on the hillside, bathed in the valley stream, and lolled in the shade of magnolias, "disclosing their beauties in the fluttering breeze."

The thirty-six-year-old naturalist and his companion, a young trader, watched unseen as the girls chased each other and crushed on their lips and cheeks the wild strawberries they had been collecting. Overcome by the "delicious scene," the two voyeurs crept down the hill in hopes of joining in the frolic of the "Cherokee virgins." A guard of Indian matrons discovered them and gave the alarm. The virgins scattered. Bartram and the trader ran like satyrs and cut off a group of them, who took shelter in a grove and peeped through the bushes at their panting approach. Something about these white interlopers must have signaled honorable intentions, for after a few moments the "sylvan nymphs" stepped into the open and shyly advanced on the two men, holding out baskets of strawberries and "merrily telling us their fruit was ripe and sound."

Whatever Bartram's description may say about the state

William Bartram, drawn from a portrait painted by Charles Willson Peale in 1808, when the botanist was 49 and tending his garden on the Schuylkill, his years of wandering long behind him.

of his libido — the scene of "primitive innocence," he admitted, proved "too enticing for hearty young men" to look on as "idle speculators" — it stands as an outstanding example of his philosophy of nature. Apparently he had never read Rousseau, but his schooling at the Philadelphia Academy had acquainted him with Pope and Addison and their idealized view of uncorrupted nature. The natural world to Bartram was "inexpressibly beautiful and pleasing" and its native inhabitants lived in a state of grace. The wild America that Bartram roamed from 1773 through 1776 presented in its "amplitude and magnificence" no less than "an idea of the first appearance of the earth to man at the creation."

William Bartram shared with his father, John Bartram, a fascination with the natural world, but otherwise they couldn't have been more different — the one dreamy, romantic, rhapsodic, the other flinty, practical, laconic.

The elder Bartram, whom Linnaeus called "the greatest natural botanist in the world," was a self-educated Quaker farmer whose early field trips through eastern Pennsylvania, the Catskill Mountains, coastal New Jersey, Maryland, and Virginia were made only after the fall harvest was in. Although something of an ethnographer, he had little use for native Americans. Indians had killed his father while homesteading on the Carolina frontier in 1709, and their uprisings occasionally interfered with his explorations.

John Bartram was born in Darby, outside Philadelphia, in 1699. His interest in botany may have been kindled at an early age by his father, a farmer and lay doctor who ministered to his Quaker neighbors with medicines concocted from local herbs. An oft-told tale credits the intricate structure of a daisy — plucked and examined by Bartram as a young man while ploughing a field — for inspiring his botanical pursuits. According to this account, he went shortly afterward to Philadelphia to purchase books on botany and a Latin grammar to train himself in the language of science.

The story may be apocryphal; whatever the inspiration, John started collecting the seeds of wild plants and by 1730 had begun the botanical garden on the Schuylkill River that made him, with his friend Benjamin Franklin, one of the two most important figures in eighteenth-century American science. He attracted influential friends and patrons. James Logan, who as secretary to William Penn had arrived in Philadelphia the year of Bartram's birth, opened his library — the best in the Colonies — for his young friend's use. Two wealthy English Quakers, the merchant Peter Collinson and physician Dr. John Fothergill, signed on as Bartram's patrons and sponsored many of the expeditions he made over the next forty years. Collinson mentored the colonial farmer, introducing him by letter to Linnaeus and other European botanists, correcting his grammar, sending him books and magazines, and even advising him on what clothes to wear as a guest in the homes of Virginia gentry.

William and his twin sister, Elizabeth, were born in 1739, the fifth and sixth children of nine sired by John with his second wife, Ann. (John had two children by his first wife, Mary, who died in 1727.)

From childhood, nature and drawing were Billy's consuming passions. His father encouraged him by letting him draw on Sundays. John's fellow Quakers must have frowned on this sacrilegious indulgence. Later, the elder Bartram's freely expressed deistic views got him expelled from the Darby Meeting. Characteristically, he continued to attend anyway.

William typified the well-born child of a man who had come up the hard way. Where John had minimal schooling, his son benefited from the best education available, at Franklin's Philadelphia Academy. Where the father by hard work and good business sense increased his land holdings and became a prosperous farmer, William showed no inclination for either farming or commerce and whiled away his youth reading, shooting, and drawing birds and plants. John worried about his son's ability to earn a living and in 1761 packed him off, at age twenty-one, to Cape Fear, North Carolina, to set up in merchandising under the watchful eye of an uncle. The experience didn't take, and Billy's business floundered. He also fell into unrequited love with a widowed cousin, and when his father passed through on his way south in 1765, the son forsook his troubles to join him on his journey.

John had recently been appointed botanist to King George III, and the £50 stipend that went with the job was enough to finance a field trip to Georgia and Florida, remote regions he had longed to visit. He was sixty-six years old and suffered from fever, jaundice, diarrhea, and possibly typhoid through much of the five-month journey, and when returning to Philadelphia by ship he was badly seasick.

Despite these infirmities, John Bartram's curiosity never flagged. He filled his journal with detailed descriptions of the region's soil, fossils, springs, plants, animals, and Indians and kept a daily record of weather conditions until he broke his thermometer while climbing a tree to raid a bee colony for honey. Together the Bartrams ascended the St. John's River four hundred miles to its sources — the first white men to do so. Among the many flora they discovered was the *Franklinia alatamaha* (named after Ben), a flowering shrub they found growing on the Altamaha River in Georgia. Although widely cultivated, it has not been seen in the wild since 1803.

This was the last and greatest journey of John Bartram's fruitful life. The adventure proved memorable to his son as well. Against John's better judgment, William decided to stay on in Florida and try his hand as an indigo planter on the St. John's. It was a disastrous enterprise. William turned out to be even more inept at farming than he had been at business. A family friend visited him in August 1766 and reported back to his father on "the forlorn state of poor Billy Bartram." This "gentle, mild young man" lived in a "hovel" with "no wife, no friend, no companion, no neighbour, no human inhabitant within nine miles," poorly provisioned and in fever much of the time, working the land with six slaves who were "rather plagues than aids to him, of whom one is so insolent as to threaten his life, one a useless expense, one a helpless child in arms." William returned to Philadelphia the following winter and, no doubt to his father's chagrin, hired himself out as a day laborer. In 1771 he moved back to Cape Fear, opened his business again — and sank heavily into debt. His father bailed him out and that same year prudently deeded his garden to William's brother, John Jr.

BILLY'S STAR WOULD SOON RISE. He stayed on at Cape Fear through 1772, sending occasional drawings to Dr. Fothergill, his father's old patron, who, despite reservations, agreed to finance another trip that William proposed through the Carolinas, Georgia, and Florida. Fothergill would pay him £50 a year, plus extra for drawings, and in return William would send him seeds of new plants for his Essex garden.

The arrangement proved felicitous. Fothergill got his seeds, and William flowered into his full potential as a naturalist and writer. From his four years of wandering came Bartram's *Travels*, his lasting contribution to the literature of nature. A work of idiosyncratic genius, it wedded a romantic vision to a keen descriptive eye, and the fantastic world portrayed would find its way into some of the great poetry of his age.

Bartram returned briefly to Philadelphia; then, bidding his parents goodbye, he set sail for Charleston in March 1773. His brigantine rode out storms and cut through moonlit seas. Bartram thrilled to the sight of whales and porpoises and immense flights of migrating birds. He inhaled the windborne fragrance of flowering trees wafting from the wild shore. Who could guess what discoveries lay beyond it?

He did not linger long in Charleston but proceeded to Savannah, the sooner to begin his explorations. Over the next year Bartram toured virtually all of coastal Georgia and much of the colony's interior. He ventured up the "peaceful Alatamaha," retracing the steps he and his father had taken eight years before, and followed the St. Mary's to its source in the Okefenokee Swamp. He ascended the Savannah River to the fall line in Augusta, hiked overland to the Cherokee settlements near present-day Athens, turned northeast to the confluence of the Tugaloo and Seneca rivers, returned via the Savannah to its namesake city, and set off to St. Simon's Island for embarkation to Florida. Bartram traveled on foot and horseback and by canoe; alone, with a single companion and — in his backwoods peregrinations through Indian country — in the company of militia. He rubbed shoulders with Creek and Cherokee chiefs, frontiersmen, traders, planters, and colonial administrators. At St. Simon's he idled in the company of a hermitic beekeeper, picnicking on venison and brandied honeywater to the serenade of mockingbirds and painted buntings.

Bartram departed by ship from Fort Fredericka in April 1774, bound for his old haunts on the St. John's River in what was then called East Florida. Reports of Indian attacks on the river's upper trading post forced the captain to turn back, and Bartram was put ashore to make his own way south. He soon found a friendly planter who was heading to St. Augustine on business and agreed to take him by boat to Cowford (Jacksonville), where he procured a small sailboat for further travel.

The St. John's rises out of its swampy headwaters above Lake Okeechobee and drains much of central Florida in a northerly meander to its outlet near the Georgia border. It is a big river, several miles across through much of its lazy run to sea, lined with cypress, palms, and live-oaks festooned with Spanish moss, and opening up at several points into wide, shallow lakes. Along the river traveled by the naturalist, grapevines as thick as a man's leg weaved among the treetops. Orange trees, brought to Florida by Spaniards two centuries before, grew wild on ridges, their blossoms sweetening the morning air.

When thunderstorms forced Bartram ashore, he huddled under the boat's sail until they passed. Ascending the river once more on a freshening breeze, he watched egrets and ibises stalking frogs along the banks. Pelicans plummeted into the river, exploding in spray and rising ponderously with their catch, while flocks of sandhill cranes wheeled overhead, filling the sky with their "musical clangour."

South of Fort Picolata, Bartram observed a spectacle associated more with northern trout streams than semitropical rivers — "innumerable millions" of mayflies rising from the water near the banks and fluttering upstream on diaphanous wings. In the space of a few minutes the mayflies performed their nuptial dance, dropped their fertilized eggs on the water, and died. Bartram saw their brief metamorphosis from homely subsurface insects to airborne creatures of exquisite delicacy — "the only space of their life that admits of pleasure and enjoyment" — as an object lesson in "the vanity of our own pursuits."

IMPELLED, AS HE PUT IT, "by a restless spirit of curiosity," Bartram in his four years of wandering added numerous discoveries to the taxonomic lists, including the royal palm, yellowroot, oil nut, oakleaf hydrangea, and golden primrose. He also described in detail all manner of fish, frogs, snakes, tortoises, lizards, mammals, and birds.

And alligators. Two centuries after he wrote of it, Bartram's hyperbolic and near-hysterical account of the American alligator remains unique:

> Behold him rushing forth from the flags and reeds. His enormous body swells. His plaited tail brandished high, floats upon the lake. The waters like a cataract descend from his opening jaws. Clouds of smoke issue from his dilated nostrils. The earth trembles with his thunder.

The first of several encounters between Bartram and alligators occurred just upstream from Lake Dexter on the upper St. John's. He had moored his boat and camped on a promontory with a "free prospect of the river, which was a matter of no trivial consideration to me, having good reason to dread the subtle attacks of the alligators, who were crowding about my harbour." Despite this ominous gathering, Bartram decided to row to a nearby lagoon to fish for his supper. Prudently leaving behind his gun, "lest I might lose it overboard in case of a battle," he armed himself with a club and set out to run the reptilian gauntlet. He was not halfway to the lagoon when the attack came and his boat nearly upset.

> My situation now became precarious to the last degree: two very large ones attacked me closely, at the same instant, rushing up with their heads and part of their bodies above the water, roaring terribly and belching floods of water over me. They struck their jaws together so close to my ears, as almost to stun me, and I expected every moment to be dragged out of the boat and instantly devoured.

Bartram beat off the attack and made it back to camp, where he shot one of his pursuers bold enough to follow him ashore. At dusk he gazed across the river. The St. John's was 150 yards wide where it entered into the lake and so choked with alligators, he breathlessly declared, "it would have been easy to have walked across on their heads." The alligators had formed a phalanx across the inlet to intercept fish on their migratory passage downriver — "from shore to shore, and perhaps half a mile above and below me ... one solid bank of fish."

> I have seen an alligator take up out of the water several great fish at a time, and just squeeze them betwixt his jaws, while the tails of the great trout flapped about his eyes and lips, ere he had swallowed them. The horrid noise of their closing jaws, their plunging amidst the broken banks of fish, and rising with their prey some feet upright above the water, the floods of water and blood rushing out of their mouths, and the clouds of vapour issuing from their wide nostrils, were truly frightful.

Bartram watched the bloody melee until the light faded, and listened through the night to the slapping and churning of jaws drifting up through the orange trees. The revelation that the alligators were after fish filled him with relief, and except for a visit from two bears drawn by the smell of his cook pot, the night passed uneventfully.

It is said that Bartram heard the bellowing of alligators in nightmares for the rest of his life. *Travels* records other alligator attacks, but characteristically Bartram's curiosity proved stronger than his fear, and he did not hesitate to go ashore to examine their cone-like nests along the banks. His melodramatic accounts were ridiculed after *Travels* appeared in 1791 — alligators, at least near human settlements, were not known to be so aggressive — although later explorers of the upper St. John's confirmed that he had not been exaggerating in his description of them in a wild state.

Bartram dallied in the wilderness of the upper St. John's, "under the care of the Almighty, and protected by the invisible hand of my guardian angel." Aside from alligators, wolves, and mosquitoes, it was a benevolent wilderness. He went as far as New Smyrna on the coast and, returning downriver, made a side trip to Salt Springs. This "amazing crystal fountain," one of many he visited in the limestone country of central Florida, enchanted him as he watched it surging from an underwater cavern and flowing through six miles of meadows into Lake George. The water of these "Elysian springs" was so clear as not to exist. He watched the brightly colored fish "sailing or floating like butterflies in the cerulean ether." Since each species of fish kept to itself and he saw no evidence of predation, it appeared to Bartram as an aquatic peaceable kingdom.

No plant or animal seems to have escaped his investigation. Testing the deep purple fruit of the tree-like Indian fig cactus, he found it a powerful diuretic that turned his urine the same deep purple. Softshell turtles, "extremely fat and delicious" (and purgative if eaten to excess) provided a bountiful feast as well as an audience of vultures and ravens waiting for the pickings.

Joining a trading caravan heading inland, he paused to study the dens of gopher tortoises burrowed into the sandy hills of Florida's central highlands and became the first naturalist to describe them.

Riding west and north from Lake George through the oak and pine forests, the caravan arrived on the shores of what is now Orange Lake, south of Gainesville. Bartram and his companions were greeted by Indians, and in the lodge of the chief they passed the calumet and a bowl of ceremonial gruel. The elderly chief, called the Cowkeeper — "a tall well-made man, very affable and cheerful ... his eyes lively and full of fire" — took an instant liking to Bartram and gave him carte blanche to range his country in search of specimens. He also bestowed on the naturalist the name by which the Creeks and Seminoles would know him: *Puc Puggy*, the Flower Hunter.

Bartram's account of the Creeks and their tribal kin, the Seminoles, reflects his benign attitude toward America's native inhabitants. In his detailed descriptions of Indian life and customs he showed himself an ethnographer of the first order. Aware of painting perhaps too rosy a picture of Florida's Indians in their state of nature, "free from want or desire," he attempted also to present their weaknesses. These he saw as a propensity to war, slavery, and sexual license; but as he quickly added, they seemed no worse in these regards than whites.

The Creeks had existed on the fringes of Spain's colonial empire for two centuries (the Spaniards settled St. Augustine in 1565 and ceded Florida to Britain in 1763). By the time Bartram encountered the Creeks, their culture had been heavily influenced by European contact: crucifixes hung from wampum collars, and they herded horses and cattle on the rolling Alachua Savannah. Civilization had not debased them, however. Bartram admired their fierce independence, noting that while many were baptized and Spanish-speaking, "yet they have been the most bitter and formidable Indian enemies the Spanish ever had." The Upper Creeks, or Muscogulges, had cut the old Spanish Road between St. Augustine on the Atlantic and St. Marks on the Gulf of Mexico, restricting white settlement to the coasts. The Lower Creeks, or Seminoles, while "a weak people with respect to numbers," controlled virtually all of the peninsula's swampy interior.

Bartram would never know the fate of these two nations, although his observation that they had nothing to fear "but the gradual encroachments of the white people" suggests that he might have guessed. The Creeks, defeated by Andrew Jackson at the Battle of Horseshoe Bend, in 1814, were sold into slavery and extirpated as a tribe. Years later, when Jackson was president, he ordered the Seminoles, along with the Cherokees and Choctaws, removed beyond the Mississippi so whites could settle their lands. But for the Seminoles there would be no Trail of Tears. Beset by U.S. troops, they withdrew into the tractless Everglades — a region, as Bartram described it, "cut and divided into thousands of islets, knolls, and eminences, by the innumerable rivers, lakes, swamps, vast savannas and ponds" — and fought them to a standoff.

Continuing west, Bartram in June 1774 visited the Suwannee, Florida's main river on the Gulf Coast. It struck him as a wild and alluring country as he stood on an arm of high ground and looked across "the most extensive cane break" on earth. Bartram rued civilization's destructive impulses and was critical, for instance, of English planters who tore out groves of feral orange trees to sow corn and indigo, but as a Quaker he believed man and nature could live in harmony. Noting the region's fair climate and rich soil, he foresaw a time when the land under cultivation would become "rich, populous, and delightful." This sentiment would be echoed later when, crossing the "great and beautiful Alachua Savanna," he mused that it might someday support thousands in a rural utopia.

After his Suwannee sojourn, Bartram returned with the caravan to the upper trading post on the St. John's, where he found a large party of Seminoles camped nearby. Fortified with twenty kegs of rum traded for horses at St. Augustine, the Indians went on a ten-day drunk and were joined by most of the white traders and their women. Bartram and a Seminole chief known as the Long Warrior were among the few to abstain. It is in character for Bartram that he in no way condemned the bacchanal except to call it "ludicrous." He watched with amusement a "comic farce" played out within the larger spectacle as the women, refraining from swallowing the rum pushed on them by the reeling traders, instead spat it into bottles secreted in their blouses. After the regular supply ran out, this "precious cordial" was resold at scalper's prices.

A curious incident occurred soon afterward, and this time Bartram could not avoid participating. He was sitting alone in the council house, drawing specimens, when he heard a commotion from the Indian lodges beyond the stockade. An interpreter told him that a large rattlesnake had invaded the encampment. The Indians were loathe to kill the rattler, fearing its spirit would influence others snakes to seek revenge, and wanted Bartram to do the job for them. "Apprehending some disagreeable consequences," the naturalist begged off and tried to sneak out the back of the council house when three Seminoles approached, calling for Puc Puggy. They prevailed upon him, and Bartram went reluctantly to their camp. He found the rattler, a gigantic diamondback, slithering between campfires, forked tongue working, while the Indians cowered at a distance. When Bartram confronted the snake it coiled into a striking pose, but he quickly dispatched it. He then cut off its head and returned with it to the council house, where he removed the fangs and added them to his collection. For his action the Seminoles declared Puc Puggy a "worthy and brave warrior." Puc Puggy himself thought the rattlesnake "a wonderful creature" and regretted killing it.

Bartram departed his beloved East Florida in September 1774. He spent the winter in Charleston, and in April of the following year set out for the Cherokee country and the lands beyond the mountains. Over the next two years he explored western Georgia and North Carolina, West Florida, and southern Alabama and Mississippi. He was happy enough in his further journeys, but his spirit of exploration had begun to flag. Alone in the Nantahala Mountains (shortly after his idyll with the Cherokee virgins), he recalled his stay among the "amiable and polite inhabitants of Charleston" and compared himself to Nebuchadnezzar, "expelled from the society of men, and constrained to roam in the mountains and wilderness, there to herd and feed with the wild beasts of the forest." The Bible he carried throughout his travels may have mitigated his loneliness but could do nothing for the physical problems that now beset him. His eyes became alarmingly inflamed, laying him up for five weeks. The illness disrupted his itinerary and was serious enough to convince him to return home.

Bartram arrived in Philadelphia in January 1777. No doubt he had many stories to tell his aged father about their old stomping grounds in East Florida. John Bartram must have listened eagerly to these accounts and been cheered as well by the knowledge that his son had developed into a first-rate naturalist. Father and son would have eight more months together before John's death the following September, at age seventy-eight. The Revolutionary War had begun during William's absence, and British troops had recently occupied the city. John's family believed his death was hastened by fear of what the soldiers might do to his garden. (They left it untouched.)

William settled into civilized life. Drawing from copious notes compiled over four years of exploration, he eventually set to work writing the *Travels*, which was published in 1791 in Philadelphia and came out the following year in London. (Full title: *Travels Through North & South Carolina, Georgia, East & West Florida, the Cherokee Country, the Extensive Territories of the Muscogulges, or Creek Confederacy, and the Country of the Choctaws.*) By 1801 it had been translated into German, Dutch, and French and had run through seven European editions. The book drew mixed reviews at home but proved an instant success abroad. Perhaps Bartram's lyrical rendering of the American wilderness was too much for his utilitarian countrymen, who still looked upon the continent's wild reaches as something to conquer, not to celebrate.

To Europeans his descriptions were literally fantastic, and they influenced a generation of young poets. A dream may truly have inspired Samuel Taylor Coleridge, as he claimed, to write *Kubla Khan*, but it was Bartram's *Travels* that inspired the dream itself. The poet's Alph the sacred river, surging from "caverns measureless to man" and "meandering with a mazy motion / Through wood and dale" came right out of Bartram's description of central Florida's limestone hydrology, while the "many an incense-bearing tree" and "forests ancient as the hills / Enfolding sunny spots of greenery" were lifted from his account of the Nantahala Mountains. Likewise, the rumblings of the thunderstorm in *The Rime of the Ancient Mariner* were first recorded by Bartram on his wilderness journeys. William Wordsworth's pastoral scenes in *Ruth* and his nature passages in *Prelude* — indeed, his entire philosophy of natural harmony and religion of nature — show

Bartram's influence as well. His descriptive passages also echo in the works of Robert Southey and the French poet Chateaubriand, who commandeered long sections of Bartram's work for *Atala* and *Le Voyage en Amerique.*

Travels was important for more than its literary influence. As a work of natural history it made significant contributions to botany, zoology, and ethnography. Bartram catalogued 215 species of American birds — the most complete list to that time — and wrote the first serious study of their migratory habits, while his voluminous writings about the Creeks, Seminoles, and Choctaws still have value to historical anthropologists.

Although the self-effacing naturalist did not intend it, *Travels* remains above all a monument to its author. In the words of his biographer Ernest Earnest, "There is a strong lyric quality that makes the *Travels* throughout a revelation of the personality of William Bartram."

Bartram, who never married, assumed his father's role as an elder in the American scientific community. He counted Thomas Jefferson among his friends, and other luminaries who came to see his famous garden included Alexander Hamilton, James Madison, and George Washington (who, expecting something more formal, was not impressed). The garden became a focal point for a younger generation of naturalists and helped sustain Philadelphia's pre-eminence in the natural sciences. Bartram encouraged many fledgling naturalists who would later gain fame, among them the entomologist Thomas Say (a grand-nephew), the botanists Benjamin Smith Barton and Thomas Nuttall, and the ornithologist Alexander Wilson.

William Bartram lived until 1823. He was eighty-four when he died, suddenly, at home on a summer morning, after completing an article on the natural history of a plant.

3

George Drouillard: Lewis & Clark's Indispensable Man

MIDWAY THROUGH THEIR 28-MONTH-LONG JOURNEY TO THE Pacific Ocean and back, the members of the Lewis and Clark expedition spent the cold, wet winter of 1806 at the mouth of the Columbia River. The soggy weather — it rained all but twelve days during their stay — added to the tedium of camp life, and the explorers passed much of the time scratching fleas and waiting for spring. Many of the expedition's members were in poor health, suffering from colds, rheumatism, boils, dysentery, and venereal infections picked up from the local Indians. Food offered about the only variety in their dreary lives, for the Columbia's estuary and headlands provided a bountiful fare. They ate anchovies, salmon, sturgeon, porpoise ("disagreeable," noted Meriwether Lewis in his journal), the blubber of beached whales ("pallitable and tender"), and the flesh of such land creatures as otter, beaver, dog, and mule deer. But day in and day out, their staple diet was elk — lean, tough, winter elk, which they ate boiled and flavored with salt distilled from seawater.

The chief provider of elk, as well as most of the other wild creatures that nourished them, was George Drouillard, the expedition's civilian hunter and sign-language interpreter. Next to the leadership of Meriwether Lewis and William Clark (who in their journals invariably spelled his name phonetically as "Drewyer"), the expedition's success rested on Drouillard's wilderness prowess and skill with a rifle. Lewis described how six Clatsop

Indians "witnessed Drewyer's shooting ... , which has given them a very exalted opinion of us as marksmen." With his inimitable style and spelling, William Clark noted how one morning he "sent out Drewyer and one man to hunt, they returned in the evening Drewyer haveing killed 7 elk; I scercely know how we Should Subsist, I beleive but badly if it was not for the exertions of this excellent hunter."

George Drouillard learned to hunt and track while growing up on the frontier of the old Northwest Territory, in what is now Michigan and Illinois. His mother was a Shawnee. His father, a French-Canadian employed as an interpreter at Detroit, a hub of the fur trade, was probably part Indian. Little is known of Drouillard's ancestry, but he must have come from a long line of voyageurs. In the employ of French and British fur companies in the seventeenth and eighteenth centuries, these legendary wilderness travelers had blazed a trail by stream, lake, and portage across most of Canada. Given this legacy of exploration and adventure, Drouillard must have jumped at the chance offered by Lewis to sign on with the Corps of Discovery.

Lewis, a captain in the U.S. Army, had been charged by President Thomas Jefferson to trace the Missouri River to its source in the "Stony Mountains" and then to descend the Columbia River to the Pacific. When Lewis was preparing for the expedition in the fall of 1803, he found Drouillard working as a hunter and interpreter at Fort Massac, an army post on the lower Ohio River, and hired him for $25 a month. Lewis's notes are silent on what attracted him to Drouillard, but the young man fit perfectly his prescription for an able recruit. As he advised Clark, when choosing men for the expedition, avoid "young gentlemen"; instead, pick backwoodsmen with wilderness know-how, "capable of bearing bodily fatigue in a pretty considerable degree."

The expedition was a military operation, and most of the men recruited for it came from army units stationed at posts on the Ohio. Civilians who signed on were required to enlist, but

George Drouillard, Lewis and Clark's ace hunter and sign-language interpreter. The drawing is conjectural, as there is no known portrait made of him in his lifetime.

Lewis made an exception for Drouillard — perhaps at his request, but more likely because of the special nature of his job. He was exempted from guard duty and other routine camp chores, and his monthly pay was five times more than a private's.

In May 1804, after wintering on the Wood River in Illinois, the explorers proceeded up the Missouri in a 55-foot keelboat and two pirogues. They were bound for the villages of the Mandan Sioux, 1,600 miles upstream, at the Great Bend of the Missouri, where they would build a stockade (Fort Mandan) and pass the winter before crossing the Rockies. At this point the party comprised forty-six men, a number that included a dozen boatmen hired only for the first leg of the journey. They averaged ten hard miles a day. Although the boats were equipped with sails, getting them upriver depended mainly on toil and sweat. The men rowed or poled or waded waist-deep in the current, hauling them at the end of rawhide ropes.

They worked up prodigious appetites honed to razor sharpness by the fierce prairie sun and wind. The job of keeping their bellies stoked fell to Drouillard and sometimes one or two other men dispatched each morning to shoot game. In a poorer environment their job might have been daunting, but the Missouri country teemed with game. The bottomlands along the lower part of the river were thick with whitetail deer. Black bears were also numerous and easy picking — in the span of one week Drouillard killed four. By early August, the expedition had passed the mouth of the Platte River and began encountering large herds of buffalo. In this land of plenty, Clark celebrated his thirty-fourth birthday with a feast of venison, elk, and beaver tail (a particular delicacy), topped off with a dessert of wild cherries, plumbs, raspberries, grapes, and currants.

The supplies carried by Lewis and Clark included flour, cornmeal, and salt pork. They foraged for berries, greens, and other edible plants. (Foraging was a specialty of Sacagawea, the Shoshone woman who with her husband, Toussaint Charbonneau, joined them at Fort Mandan.) They traded with the Mandans for beans and corn and with Columbia River tribes for dried salmon. Using cut bait and handlines, they caught catfish and trout. All these were but minor additions to a diet that would make a modern nutritionist blanche: for all practical purposes the explorers' "four basic food groups" were meat, meat, meat, and meat.

The corps of discovery departed Fort Mandan in April 1805, following the Missouri due west into the High Plains. The party now consisted of thirty-two adults, one child (Sacagawea's baby, Pompey), and a dog (Lewis's Newfoundland, named Seaman). To their astonishment, game was even more plentiful than it had been on the lower river. It was also easier to kill: "We can ... obtain whatever species of meat the country affords in as large quantity as we wish," observed Lewis. (On the return journey, descending the Yellowstone River, Clark wrote, "The Buffalow and Elk is astonishingly noumerous" and "So jintle that we frequently pass within 20 or 30 paces of them without their being the least alarmd.") Their meticulous records show that in one stretch of seventy-eight days (April 27–July 14, 1805) hunters brought in 115 deer, 87 bison, 63 elk, 27 antelope, 14 grizzly bears, and 9 bighorn sheep.

Lewis put the matter simply: "We eat an emensity of meat." He found that the dressed meat from a single buffalo, or from one elk and a deer, or from four deer could feed the party for an entire day. Ken Walcheck, a Montana wildlife biologist and student of the expedition, has analyzed the explorers' data and confirmed earlier estimates that they each consumed eight to ten pounds of meat a day, roughly six thousand calories per man.

Nearly every entry of Lewis and Clark's journals mentions food, and the references to meat often note whether it was lean or fat. The explorers craved fat: no surprise, considering the calories they must have been burning. They especially loved the fatty, sweet flesh of beaver, which reminded them of pork. About the only thing better was the greasy, succulent flesh of dogs supplied by the Mandans and later the Chinooks. Lewis admitted becoming "extreemly fond" of fresh puppy and claimed that the men enjoyed their best health when it was a major part of their diet. Clark, for one, never acquired the taste.

The richest buffalo meat came from a young cow or calf. A bull was apt to be so lean that only the tongue and marrow bones were taken and the rest left for the wolves. The choicest parts of a buffalo carcass — the flesh of the hump and the fat around the kidney — were the main ingredients of *boudin blanc.* Lewis lovingly described the making of this prairie delicacy, a specialty of Toussaint Charbonneau. He started with a few a feet of lower gut, squeezed out the excrement, and tied off one end. Next, he pounded the hump meat and kidney fat together with flour, salt, and pepper into a pudding. He then stuffed the pudding into the gut and tied off the other end to make a sausage. This he "baptised" in the Missouri "with two dips and a flirt," threw into a kettle to boil, and finished off by frying in bear grease. The result, wrote Lewis, was a meal guaranteed to assuage "the pangs of a keen appetite."

With buffalo and elk so plentiful on the plains, shooting them wasn't much sport. Other game proved more challenging. The quicksilver speed of pronghorn antelopes and their ability to stay out of reach of his gun astonished Lewis. One morning, he and two other hunters (one of whom was probably Drouillard) spent several hours stalking a buck and his harem of six does. Twice they managed to get close enough for a shot, only to see their prey bound away. The pronghorns always took the highest and most open ground, the better to spot danger with their telescopic eyes. On the hunters' second attempt, the only approach that offered any cover was directly upwind; they sneaked within two hundred yards before the pronghorns got whiff of them and fled, dropping into a ravine and reappearing on a hillside three miles away. They had covered the distance so quickly that, at first, Lewis didn't believe it — no animal could run so fast. His doubts vanished when the pronghorns took off again, their fleetness recalling "reather the rappid flight of birds than the motion of quadrupeds."

Nor did the explorers fare well with bighorn sheep, which they began seeing on the bluffs and cliffs overlooking the Missouri after leaving Fort Mandan. Although sheep were plentiful, in more than three months ascending the river they bagged only five, two shot by Drouillard and one each by Lewis, Clark, and William Bratton, another of the corps's more able hunters. Drouillard had the distinction of shooting the first bighorn, a ram with a head and horns weighing twenty-seven pounds.

Of all the animals they encountered, none got their adrenaline pumping more than the grizzly bear. After Lewis rather easily killed a young male of about three hundred pounds, he decided that Mandan accounts of the bear's ferocity were exaggerated — "they are by no means as formidable or dangerous as they have been represented." His blithe assessment changed quickly enough. A few days later, Drouillard and Clark pumped ten balls into an old boar grizzly before it dropped. The carcass weighed an estimated six hundred pounds. Clark declared it "a turrible animal . . . verry hard to kill." Lewis was awed by the size of its heart, as big as an ox's.

A week later, six of the men — "all good hunters," according to Lewis — spied a grizzly some distance from the river and approached within forty yards before opening fire. A volley of four balls ripped into the bear. It wheeled and charged, took two more rounds from a second volley, and kept on coming. One ball broke the animal's shoulder, slowing it slightly, but even so it was on them faster than they could believe.

The terrified men ran pell-mell toward the river. Two made it to a canoe while the other four took cover in a clump of willows, hastily reloaded, and fired again. When the bear chased after two of them, they flung aside their rifles and plunged down a twenty-foot embankment into the water.

The enraged grizzly tumbled after them. Finally, one of the hunters on the bank put a bullet through its brain, killing it instantly. After dragging the bear ashore and butchering it, they counted eight balls in its carcass. The bear "being old the flesh was indifferent," Lewis noted. "They therefore took only the skin and fleece, the latter made for us several gallons of oil."

As the expedition approached the Great Falls of the Missouri, Lewis complained that bears had become so "troublesome that I do not think it prudent to send one man alone on an errand of any kind." On one occasion, Drouillard was chased a hundred yards after shooting a bear through the heart. Another man barely escaped a grizzly's wrath by diving into the river — the most common, if dubious, means of escape — and hiding beneath an undercut bank.

Lewis used a similar tactic when charged by a bear. Disregarding his own advice, he had gone out alone to hunt and had just shot a buffalo when he noticed a grizzly approaching, just twenty steps away. He raised his gun to shoot but realized he hadn't reloaded. With the bear at his heels, he took off across the plain and plunged into a shallow part of the river. Standing at waist depth, he drew his knife and turned to face his pursuer. To his bafflement and relief, the bear drew up at the bank, then wheeled in retreat and galloped off at full tilt in the opposite direction.

"I felt myself not a little gratified that he had declined the combat," wrote Lewis in his journal. In place of his earlier dismissal of grizzlies was a new respect: "I must confess that I do not like the gentlemen and had reather fight two Indians than one bear."

In all, the explorers had a dozen encounters with aggressive silvertips, and it was sheer luck that no one was killed or mauled. Yet at times they couldn't resist having a little sport with them. At the Great Falls, Drouillard and a dozen others invited danger by entering a willow thicket to flush a bruin. Was it chance or his superior hunter's instincts that put Drouillard face to face with the grizzly in its lair? He heard a branch crack and fired at the brown mass that burst upon him. The bullet passed through the heart but had little immediate effect. The grizzly crashed from the willows and sprinted a hundred yards before collapsing.

A grizzly's ability to hold up against murderous fire seems not to have shaken the explorers' confidence in their weapons. Some of them — almost certainly including Drouillard, as well as Lewis and Clark — carried the Pennsylvania (or Kentucky) long rifle, the premier hunting arm of its day. The expedition's manifest also lists fifteen government-issue rifles, prototypes of the army's Model 1803. They were manufactured at the U.S. arsenal at Harper's Ferry, along with spare parts, bullet molds, 400 pounds of lead, and 200 pounds of black powder. Compared to a typical long rifle, the Model 1803 had a shorter, thicker barrel (allowing a heavier powder load) and a larger caliber (.52 versus .40), qualities that made it the superior rifle for big game.

On its homeward journey from the Pacific, the expedition split up near what is now Missoula, Montana, with Clark veering south to explore the Yellowstone while Lewis continued east to pick up the Missouri. In July 1806, at the mouth of the Marias River (named for a lady friend), Lewis left his main party and took Drouillard and two others he especially trusted, the brothers Joseph and Rueben Field, to reconnoiter this tributary. It was here, after coming upon a band of eight Blackfeet, that the Corps of Discovery had its only serious confrontation with Indians. Outnumbered two to one, Lewis made the best of this worrisome situation, presenting gifts and parleying with the warriors around a common campfire; with his command of sign language, Drouillard did the interpreting. Lewis posted a watch, then fell into a profound sleep. Early the next morning he was jolted awake by Drouillard's cursing as he struggled with one of the Blackfeet. The camp was in pandemonium — the Indians were attempting to steal their guns and horses. In the ensuing melee, Lewis shot one Blackfoot (probably fatally), and Rueben Field killed another with a knife. Lewis and his three companions drove off the warriors and rode hell-for-leather back to the Missouri to link up with the main party.

The explorers returned to civilization in September 1806, and their tales of beaver-choked streams lured other men to the Rockies. Manuel Lisa, a St. Louis fur trader, hired Drouillard to guide a party of trappers into the wilderness.

Over the next three years, Drouillard played a leading role in Lisa's efforts to build forts at the junction of the Yellowstone and Bighorn rivers and at the Three Forks, where the Jefferson, Madison, and Gallatin rivers join to form the Missouri. As an envoy to the resident Crows and the Salish (Flatheads), Drouillard was also instrumental in winning the trust of these tribes, whose friendship Lisa needed to trap in their country. The Blackfeet, their blood enemies, did not take kindly to Lisa's messing in intertribal matters. It's possible, too, that they were still angry about the fight on the Marias, and they may have remembered Drouillard as a principal in that humiliating affair. Anyway, they were truculent by nature, and the appearance of white trappers deep in their territory set them off like a swarm of hornets.

Drouillard was well aware of the danger in May 1810 when he led twenty-one of Lisa's men from the fort at Three Forks to trap the virgin waters of the Jefferson. Two trappers had been killed by Blackfeet just a few weeks before, and most were afraid to venture far beyond camp. Not so Drouillard. With a confidence born of a lifetime in the wilderness, he could more easily calculate risk and live with it. "I am too much of an Indian to be caught by Indians," he boasted. The best beaver grounds were upriver, and he convinced two other trappers (both Delaware Indians, allies of his own Shawnees) to follow him there. After the three failed to return to camp, a party went looking for them. Their worst fears were realized when they came upon the arrow-riddled bodies of the two Delawares.

As related by one of the party, farther on they found the corpse of Drouillard, lying next to his dead horse. Mangled "in a horrible manor," he had been hacked to pieces, his entrails ripped out and his head chopped off. "We saw from the marks on the ground that he must have fought in a circle on horseback, and probably killed some of his enemies, being a brave man, and well armed with a rifle, pistol, knife and tomahawk."

George Drouillard's luck had run out, but it is fitting that he died fighting in the heart of the wild and fiercely beautiful country he was among the first to explore. "A man of much merit," Lewis wrote of him in typically understated prose, "peculiarly useful" on their epic crossing of the continent for his knowledge of sign language and "uncommon skill as a hunter and woodsman," who encountered "all the most dangerous and trying scenes of the voyage, in which he uniformly acquitted himself with honor."

4

Going Native

FALCON'S MOTHER HAD A VISION. IT WAS WINTER, SNOW COVERED the frozen ground, and hunger gnawed at the stomachs of the band of Ottawas camped in the hills overlooking the Assiniboine River. While her children slept through the bitter night, Netnokwa prayed and sang. The next morning, she described to them how the Great Spirit had come to her, saying that today she would eat a bear. In her dream the Great Spirit had also told Netnokwa where the bear was sleeping.

Falcon listened carefully, and later that morning he loaded his musket, tied on his snowshoes, and struck out into the woods. At age thirteen, he was still learning to hunt and had yet to kill anything larger than a beaver. He told no one where he was going. His mother had said that the bear was sleeping at the edge of a meadow. After several miles he came to a clearing. It looked right, but the snow masked any obvious place for a den. He knew that sometimes you could find a hibernating bear by its condensed breath rising from the snow, but he saw no such sign. He was reconnoitering the edge of the clearing when he hit a soft spot and was suddenly up to his waist in snow. After digging out, Falcon looked down into the hole he had created and saw the head of a bear — he had fallen right into its den. Despite the disturbance, the bear slept on. The boy put the musket to its head and fired.

Back at the lodge, Netnokwa gave her son a mighty hug

when he told her the Great Spirit had fulfilled her vision: today they would eat well. Falcon's first bear called for a celebration, and according to custom, all the hunters in the band took part in the feast.

Falcon soon began to hunt in earnest, and the following summer he took his first elk. It was the start of the rut, and Falcon, crouching behind a bush, called in a large bull. His calling was rather more successful than he intended, for the bull was so big and came on so quickly that the boy lost his nerve. He dropped his gun and ran while the equally startled elk took off in the opposite direction. His buck fever quickly passed, and before long he called in a second bull and killed it.

These scenes took place two centuries ago, in what is now southern Manitoba. In most ways, Falcon was no different from any young Ottawa of this time and place. Living off the land, he and his band moved with the seasons between the western prairies and the woods and wetlands of Lake Superior. Along with elk and bear, he hunted buffalo, caribou, and moose. He trapped beavers and otters, fished for trout, walleye, and sturgeon, and harvested wild rice and the sweet sap of maples. At the posts of the Hudson's Bay Company, Falcon and his people bartered furs for powder and ball and other trade goods.

But in one respect he was very different. For "Falcon" (or *Shaw-shaw-wa-be-na-se*, as the Ottowas would have called him) had been born John Tanner, the son of white settlers in Kentucky.

Kidnapped at age nine by Ojibways, he had been taken to northern Michigan and traded to the Ottawas for blankets and tobacco. Netnokwa had lost a son and acquired Tanner to take his place in her family. Her motive was both emotional and practical, for her new son would become a hunter and help care for her in old age.

Adopting captives was universal among Indians, and since the beginning of the Stone Age it had probably been a practice common among hunter-gatherers throughout the world. A typical clan might number fewer than fifty people, and a thousand

John Tanner, a.k.a. *Shaw-shaw-wa-be-na-se*, or Falcon, was kidnapped by Ojibways on the Kentucky frontier in 1789, when he was nine years old, and raised as an Indian. As a grown man he tried but ultimately failed to reassimilate into white culture. This drawing is based on a portrait he sat for in 1828.

or so might make up an entire tribe. Disease or starvation could drive a small group to the brink of extinction, and raiding an enemy camp was a convenient way to replenish its numbers.

The colonizing of North America brought Indians and Europeans into three centuries of conflict, and in the course of that long, sad history there were many John Tanners. The threat of Indian capture was real for every frontier family. The "captivity narrative" was a staple of popular literature, and the stories of whites who had survived capture were read with a mix of fascination and horror. Both Indians and Europeans raided with utter ruthlessness, and most of these accounts dwell on the savagery of Indians. But those of Tanner and a few others are sympathetic toward their captors, whose society offered freedoms and a degree of tolerance unknown among whites.

THE HISTORICAL RECORD SHOWS that, indeed, many whites preferred living as Indians. On the Pennsylvania-Ohio frontier in 1764, at the end of the Indian war known as Pontiac's Rebellion, the British-American victors demanded that the Shawnees and Delawares deliver up all their white captives. But to the shock of the colonials, the great majority refused to leave their Indian families. Most had been taken as children years before and by now were completely acculturated, to the extent of having forgotten English. Many had grown to adulthood, married, and had children by their Indian spouses. Some had to be bound and literally dragged back to their white relations. As historian James Axtell notes in *The European and the Indian*, a study of the clash of white and native cultures in the colonial period, the repatriated whites "responded only to Indian names, spoke only Indian dialects, felt comfortable only in Indian clothes, and in general regarded their white saviors as barbarians and their deliverance as captivity."

French colonists adapted to Indian life with even greater ease than their English counterparts. During the French and Indian War, British troops suffered many casualties at the hands of Indians led by French officers who had lived among them for years and mastered their guerrilla tactics.

Indians preferred capturing white children because they more easily adapted to tribal ways, but on occasion adults were also taken. Although frontier women lived in terror of rape by Indians, female captives were rarely sexually abused. Braves abstained from sex during periods of warfare, and incest taboos prohibited them from violating a future sister or cousin.

A captured adult male faced a more problematic future — all too often he was ceremoniously tortured and killed. But sometimes luck intervened. The life of Alexander Henry, a British trader caught up in a massacre at Fort Mackinac in 1763, was spared by a Huron brave who determined to take him into his family to replace a dead brother. Henry underwent an elaborate induction into the tribe. The Hurons shaved his head (saving a top-knot), painted his face, and decked him out in feathers, wampum collar, silver armbands, and scarlet blouse and breeches. The "ladies of the family," he later wrote, "appeared to think my person improved, and now condescended to call me handsome, even among Indians." Henry spent a year among the Hurons and found native life more pleasant than he would have imagined. He especially liked hunting raccoons with dogs: "I usually went out at the first dawn of day, and seldom returned till sunset, or till I had laden myself with as many animals as I could carry." Were it not for the lingering memory of white society, he added, "I could have enjoyed as much happiness in this as in any situation."

Daniel Boone was already wise in wilderness ways when a band of Shawnees captured him on the Licking River, in Kentucky, in 1778, and took him to their village north of the Ohio. A chief named Blackfish adopted him as his son, conferring on him the name *Sheltowee*, or Big Turtle. Boone was formally inducted into the tribe. As part of the ceremony, squaws stripped and washed him in the Scioto River — a ritual bathing that symbolically cleansed him of his white blood. In Blackfish's lodge, wrote Boone in his autobiography, he enjoyed "the affection of my new parents, brothers, sisters, and friends" and "often went a hunting with them, and frequently gained their applause" in shooting matches. (But not too much applause. On occasion he deliberately missed the target, being "careful not to exceed many of them in shooting, for no people are more envious than they in this sport.")

Boone spent four months among the Shawnees before escaping back across the Ohio and returning to his white family. But he always looked back on this interlude with nostalgia. Years later, after he settled in Missouri and the Ohio tribes began moving beyond the Mississippi, Big Turtle reconnected with his Shawnee kin and joined them on their hunts.

Unlike Henry and Boone, not every white Indian started out as a captive. From the beginning of the colonial era, "going native" appealed powerfully to people who chafed under the rules and expectations of civilization. William Penn, remarking on the allure of Indian life for some in his Quaker colony, noted that Europeans "sweat and toil" for their daily bread, while Indians appeared to live only for pleasure, passing their days "Hunting, Fishing and Fowling." Frontier whites in frequent contact with Indians observed the advantages of native life and slipped into it easily, abandoning plows and homesteads for an unfettered existence in the wilds. The colonial fathers wrung their hands over this moral degeneracy — the Puritan divine Cotton Mather blamed the Devil for luring industrious Christians into heathen idleness — and did what they could to discourage it. In 1642, the Connecticut legislature made it a crime to live like an Indian, and during King Philip's War, an Indian uprising against New England colonists in the 1670s, one white who joined his red brothers on the warpath was drawn and quartered. (Europeans could be at least as cruel as their "savage" foe.) Still the defections continued. A century later, in a book about life in the American colonies, the essayist Hector de Crèvecoeur marveled that "thousands of Europeans" had become Indians, yet "we have no example of even one of those Aborigines having from choice become Europeans!"

Living in today's urbanized environment, we can too readily romanticize the nomadic life of Indians two centuries ago. In reality it could be nasty and brutish, and dependence on game for food made eating a feast-or-famine business. At one point during his sojourn with the Shawnees, Boone subsisted for ten days on broth made from oak bark. The Shawnees had already killed and devoured all their dogs when they finally shot a deer. To prepare their shrunken stomachs for venison, they first ate a vile jelly made from the deer's guts. Big Turtle gulped down this appetizer "with wry face and disagreeable wretchings," to the amusement of his Shawnee kin.

Most of what we know about John Tanner comes from what he dictated to Dr. Edwin James, a physician who brefriended him when they were together at Fort Mackinac, where Tanner worked as an interpreter. His ghost-written account, published in 1830 as *A Narrative of the Captivity and Adventures of John*

Tanner, is a litany of hunger, exposure, disease, and the ravages of trade whiskey. Of necessity he became a passable hunter, although his many misadventures suggest he wasn't born to the chase. Once, while trying to retrieve a beaver he shot on a frozen pond, he broke through the ice and nearly drowned. Another time, he was crawling through brush to get in range of some ducks when he startled a black bear. When the bear scurried up a tree, Tanner hurriedly loaded his musket and fired. His target was directly overhead and an easy mark, but he missed it clean when the gun burst its barrel. Unsurprised by what was probably a common mishap with trade muskets, he reloaded and with a second shot knocked the bear from its perch.

With winter came a real threat of starvation, and the hunt for food took on a desperate edge. On one bitterly cold morning Tanner jumped an elk, which he then chased on snowshoes for the rest of the day and into the night before hope and strength at last failed him. His clothes were torn and stiff with frozen sweat when he began to make his way home. Stumbling through the snow, he fought off the fatal urge to lie down and sleep. For a while he lost consciousness but remained on his feet, staggering in circles. Finally he saw a light flickering in the forest, and the fire stoked by Netnokwa guided her exhausted son to their lodge.

A month later he had recovered from frostbite and was hunting with his brother when they corralled a large herd of elk at a bend in a river. The hunters killed two of the elk and drove the others onto the ice, which gave way beneath their weight. Tanner ran to the edge of the break, firing into the panicked animals. As he told James, "When my balls were all expended, I drew my knife and killed one or two with it, but all I killed in the water were in a few minutes swept under the ice, and I got none of them."

Despite the hardships and frustrations faced by Tanner and his fellow Ottawas, the freedom to move as one pleased and to live so close to nature resonated at the deepest level. The physical and spiritual worlds were one, and if the hunting was poor, old Netnokwa could summon up a vision or a bit of magic to make a ball or arrow fly straight.

Tanner tells how, one winter night when they were all hungry, Netnokwa dreamed of eating moose. The Ottawas regarded the moose, with its acute senses, as the most difficult animal to hunt. Even in a violent storm, "if a man, either with his foot or his hand, breaks even the smallest dry limb in the forest, the moose will hear it." So when she told her sons to go hunting for a moose, they complained that the air was too cold and still for stalking. Never mind, said Netnokwa — she would pray for a warm wind. For extra measure she made medicine, drawing a stick figure of a moose on birch bark, then marking the effigy with a magic goo of ground-up ocher and roots. Anything for an edge. The sons headed into the woods, and as if on cue, a breeze rose from the south. They got their moose.

Backed by Netnokwa's medicine, Tanner wound up killing seventeen moose in his best winter of hunting. "There are many Indians who hunt through the winter in that country," he said, "and kill no more than two or three moose, and some are never able to kill one."

As TANNER GREW INTO early manhood, the memory of his white childhood tugged at him. He was in regular contact with whites at trading posts and had perhaps begun to envy the life he might have had. In his thirties, on trips to Kentucky and Missouri, he connected with a long-lost brother and a sister. The reunions must have been troubling as he and his siblings struggled to bridge their cultural and linguistic divide. At the meeting with his brother they talked through an interpreter because Tanner had lost the ability to speak English, a language he eventually relearned.

Many of the personal details of his life are fuzzy, but as a young man he appears to have twice married Indian women, who bore him nine children, but neither marriage lasted. In his forties and fifties he worked as an interpreter at Fort Mackinac and at Sault Ste. Marie.

Tanner hoped that white society would accept him, but thirty years with the Ottawas had made him an Indian for good. At Sault Ste. Marie he married a white woman, but she soon left him. He eventually turned his back on the community and retreated to a cabin in the woods, lonely and increasingly bitter — "suspicious, revengeful, bad-tempered," as a contemporary recalled, and perhaps a little crazy. (At least twice he was accused of killing livestock belonging to the Baptist mission where he had previously worked.) He had a nasty falling-out with the local Indian agent and for years nursed a grudge against him. In 1846, when the agent's brother was shot and killed from ambush, many accused Tanner of the crime.

Whatever his guilt or innocence — another man ultimately confessed — Tanner chose not to put his fate at the mercy of frontier justice. He disappeared without a trace. Maybe the skeleton found years later in a nearby swamp was his, as some said. Or maybe, as others believed, he went up on the Assiniboine to live out his days with the people who knew him as Falcon.

5

The Right Stuff: Mountain Men & Voyageurs

ON A PARCHED AFTERNOON IN MAY 1834, FOUR MEN STOOD ON the Nebraska prairie around the carcass of a buffalo they had shot. Members of a fur-trade brigade bound for the Rocky Mountains, they had left the main group early that morning to hunt and had been without water for hours. The hot wind and dust and the work of butchering the buffalo under the blazing sun — propping it up, stripping back the hide, and flensing the choice meat from its hump — added to their thirst.

One of the men, a greenhorn named Townsend, suggested a dash to the Platte River for water. But the Platte was many miles away. Richardson, a seasoned mountain man and the brigade's chief hunter, knew of another source of liquid closer at hand. As Townsend related the incident later, after they rolled the buffalo over on its side, the hunter sliced into its belly, exposing the "still crawling and twisting entrails." While the greenhorn gaped in astonishment "and no little loathing," Richardson plunged his knife "into the distended paunch, from which gushed the green and gelatinous juices."

With a tin pan he strained off the water from the animal's innards, then tossed back his head and drank to the dregs this prairie elixir, "smacking his lips, and drawing a long breath after it, with the satisfaction of a man taking his wine after dinner."

Doubtless the mountain man was grandstanding some for the greenhorn's benefit. But water is where you find it, and finding it in a buffalo's guts showed the kind of resourcefulness that meant the difference between life and death on the plains.

For the mountain men of the American fur trade and for their spiritual kin, the voyageurs who plied the water routes of Canada in the employ of French and British fur companies, survival depended on resourcefulness, physical stamina, and wilderness skills acquired in the relentless pursuit of beaver.

From the Algonquian tribes along the St. Lawrence, the voyageurs adopted the birch-bark canoe as their means of penetrating into the heart of the vast continent. From the 1680s until well into the 1800s, flotillas of canoes from eastern Canada and Hudson Bay supplied a network of trading posts that eventually stretched from the Great Lakes to the Columbia and Yukon rivers.

A fur company typically signed up a voyageur for two or three years of backbreaking work. Portages, in which canoes and goods were carried overland to bypass falls and rapids, were divided into brief rest stops a third of a mile apart. A voyageur carried his load in ninety-pound packs secured to his back by a leather harness that included a forehead strap to help distribute the weight. A standard load was two packs (180 pounds), but sturdier voyageurs doubled that; bragging rights began in earnest at five packs (450 pounds), and a few Paul Bunyan types reputedly carried eight — 720 pounds. Bruised feet and sprained ankles went with the job, and more serious injuries like slipped disks and hernias could lead to paralysis or death.

Winter tested the mettle of voyageurs. Those who lived through the cold months in the wilderness boasted of their status as *hivernants* ("winterers") and looked down on the *mangeurs du lard* ("pork-eaters") who returned to the settlements in the fall. On hunting excursions or when ferrying supplies and furs between posts, voyageurs traveled by dogsled and on snowshoes. Camping at night, they made a hearth of green logs, cut long — up to twenty feet — and laid on the snow. They cut balsam branches for their beds and slept huddled together under

The mountain man Joe Walker with his Shoshone wife at the trappers' rendezvous of 1837; after a painting by Alfred Jacob Miller.

skins and blankets, feet to the fire. Burning through the night, a fire could melt a ten-foot-deep pit in the snow, and voyageurs took care not to roll into it.

Staggering under loads that would flatten a mule, paddling at forty strokes a minute for twelve to fifteen hours a day, or slogging on snowshoes through the frozen landscape, a voyageur burned more calories than a marathon runner. He lived off the land to the extent possible: depending on where he found himself, his daily ration might be measured in geese, rabbits, moose or buffalo meat, whitefish, or salmon. If game was scarce or the press of a journey left no time for hunting and fishing, he turned to staples such as dried corn and peas. If staples ran out and no fish or game could be had, the food of last resort was a variety of lichen known as *tripe de roches* ("rock tripe," so-called because it resembled chopped intestines). Boiled, it turned into a vile, viscid, foul-smelling gruel, "black and clammie & easily to be swallowed," as the trader-explorer Pierre Radisson described it.

The Indians dubbed this starvation food *windigo wakon*, after a woods spirit that out of hunger devoured its own lips.

West of Lake Winnipeg, where the forests gave way to buffalo plains, the voyageur's chief staple was pemmican. Packed with carbohydrates and protein, pemmican was the ultimate trail food. To make it, a voyageur started with strips of dried buffalo meat, called *charqui* (jerky). He removed any gristle or sinew, pounded the meat to break it down, added dried berries and melted fat, and packed the whole into a buffalo-skin bag. (As one observer noted, "hair, sticks, spruce leaves, stones, sand, etc." often found their way into the mix, too.) Sewing the bag shut made an air-tight receptacle. Thus sealed, pemmican could keep for years. Voyageurs ate it raw or cooked. A favorite meal was *rababou* — pemmican sliced and boiled with flour. After a long day of paddling and portaging, voyageurs sometimes couldn't wait for it to cool in a bowl. Instead, as one amazed witness recorded, they poured this hearty stew over a rock and licked it up like dogs.

VOYAGEURS WERE HIRED HANDS, working under contract for giant firms like the Hudson's Bay and Northwest Companies, which acquired furs by trading with Indians at posts scattered throughout the Canadian West. American fur companies didn't depend on Indians to do the trapping. At first they employed their own trappers, but the system that ultimately took hold in the Rockies relied on "free trappers." These were the mountain men of legend, like Joe Walker, Jim Bridger, Bill Sublette, Tom Fitzpatrick, and Kit Carson — independent operators who worked alone or in small groups and sold their pelts to traders at an annual trappers' rendezvous.

Rollicking bacchanals of drinking and gambling, rendezvous drew both whites and Indians and were held each summer between 1825 and 1840 along the Continental Divide, in what is now west-central Wyoming. John Kirk Townsend, the greenhorn who weeks earlier had witnessed the hunter Richardson drink from the guts of a dead bison, attended the rendezvous of 1834. He was laid up with a fever for much of the time. "There is a great variety of personages amongst us," he wrote in his journal,

> most of them calling themselves white men, French-Canadians, half-breeds, &c., their colour nearly as dark, and their manners wholly as wild, as the Indians with whom they constantly associate. These people, with their obstreperous mirth, their whooping, and howling, and quarrelling, added to the mounted Indians, who are constantly dashing into, and through our camp, yelling like fiends, the barking and baying of savage wolf-dogs, and the incessant cracking of rifles and carbines, render our camp a perfect bedlam. A more unpleasant situation for an invalid could scarcely be conceived. I am confined closely to the tent with illness, and am compelled all day to listen to the hiccoughing jargon of drunken traders, the *sacré* and *foutre* of Frenchmen run wild, and the swearing and screaming of our own men, who are scarcely less savage than the rest, being heated by the detestable liquor which circulates freely among them.

George Frederick Ruxton, an Englishman who ventured into the southern Rockies in the 1840s, never attended a rendezvous but reconstructed this scene from accounts related to him by trappers he knew:

> Seated, Indian fashion, round the fires, with a blanket spread before them, groups are seen with their "decks" of cards, playing euker, poker, and seven-up, the regular mountain games. The stakes are "beaver," which here is current coin; and when the fur is gone, their *breeches* are staked. Daring gamblers make the rounds of the camp, challenging each other to play for the trapper's highest stakes — his horse, his squaw (if he have one), and, as once happened, his scalp. "There goes hos and beaver!" is the mountain expression when any great loss is sustained; and sooner or later, "hos and beaver" invariably find their way into the insatiable pockets of the traders.

Ruxton also left us an account — one so graphic an editor refused to include it in the published version of his journal — of gastronomic sport between two trappers on the upper Arkansas River. After slaughtering a buffalo cow, Ruxton wrote, "the hunter carefully lays by, as a tidbit for himself, the 'boudins' and medullary intestine," which he prepared by partially cleaning and lightly charring over a fire.

> I once saw two Canadians commence at either end of such a coil of grease, the mess lying between them on a dirty apishamore like the coil of a huge snake. As yard after yard glided glibly down their throats, and the serpent on the saddlecloth was dwindling from an anaconda to a moderate-sized rattlesnake, it became a great point with each of the feasters to hurry his operation, so as to gain a march upon his neighbour, and improve the opportunity by swallowing more than his just proportion; each, at the same time, exhorting the other, whatever he did, to feed fair, and every now and then, overcome by the unblushing attempts of his partner to bolt a vigorous mouthful would suddenly jerk back his head, drawing out at the same moment, by the retreating motion, several yards of boudin from his neighbour's mouth and stomach — for the greasy viand required no mastication, and was bolted whole — and, snapping up himself the ravished portions, greedily swallowed them; to be in turn again withdrawn and subjected to a similar process by the other.

BECAUSE HE COULD TRADE AT the rendezvous for the few manufactured items required for survival, the free trapper had little need to visit civilization. Jim Bridger spent seventeen consecutive years in the mountains. In all that time, Old Gabe claimed, he never once tasted bread.

Anyway, who needs bread when buffalo — 40 million meals on the hoof — are there for the taking? Bridger really may have believed, as he said, that a man who ate only buffalo meat would never die. It was the mountain man's staff of life. The most tender cuts came from the hump of a young cow. Tongue was also a favorite, along with kidney fat eaten raw on the spot, sliced and dried for later consumption, or boiled down into tallow and packed in skins for a high-fat protein trail snack. The sweet, tender, fatty meat of beaver was also favored, and both the beaver's liver and tail made for a rich repast.

The mountain man varied his carnivorous diet with the fruit of wild plants (berries, grapes, plumbs, hazelnuts), lambs-quarters (a green collected along river banks), and potato-like camas roots. Both plants and animals were sources for pharmaceuticals. Powdered cornflower root mixed with water made a poultice guaranteed to cure snakebite. An all-purpose salve, good for wounds and sores and joints that ached from too many hours setting traps in frigid streams, was concocted from bear's oil and beeswax mixed with gunpowder.

In a country so bountiful the mountain man was seldom wanting, and with his basic kit — a sturdy plains rifle, tomahawk, Green River knife, and "possibles" bag filled with items of varying degree of practicality, from castoreum or "medicine" (beaver musk) for baiting traps to small bones and pebbles and similar talismans — he made the Rockies his own.

His shelter was a simple lean-to or a tipi, his bedding a blanket roll. His clothes were of buckskin, but he also wore (and preferred) cotton or wool acquired in trade at a fort or rendezvous.

A sewing kit for repairing clothes and making moccasins also came in handy for emergency medical treatment: one of the most harrowing descriptions in the literature of the fur trade is Jim Clyman's account of the impromptu plastic surgery he performed on Jedediah Smith.

In 1823, near the Black Hills, Smith was leading a party of trappers when a grizzly surprised them. As Clyman wrote in his journal, before Smith could raise his rifle the bear took him in its "capcious mouth." The grizzly threw him to the ground, breaking several ribs and nearly tearing off his scalp.

Clyman and others chased off the bear and did what they could for their leader. Blood pulsed from a gaping slash that had bared his skull, and one ear was almost severed. On Smith's orders, Clyman produced a needle and thread and began putting his boss back together, stitching "through and through and over and over laying the lacerated parts together as nice as I could." Smith pulled through and before too long was up and about.

As Clyman noted, the experience "gave us a lisson on the charcter of the grissly Barre which we did not forget."

The mountain man could make a fire any number of ways, using a bow drill like the Indians if he had to, but more likely by striking a fire-steel against a flint, sending sparks into a pile of "punk," or crumbled deadwood from a pine tree. In wet weather he might add a pinch of black powder. Once lit, he folded the smoldering punk into a bed of dry grass, then blew on the grass or waved it in the air until it ignited. Many mountain men continued to use flintlock rifles long after the introduction of percussion weapons, in part because they could double as fire starters.

The knives carried by both the mountain men and voyageurs varied in style, although most were simple trade knives manufactured in England and the eastern United States. The typical "scalper" had a six-inch blade and wooden handle. Fur companies ordered them by the hundreds of dozens at wholesale prices of less than 10 cents per knife, then sold them to trappers at trading posts or rendezvous at a thousand-percent markup. Many English knives were stamped near the handle with the initials "G.R.," for *Georgius Rex*, in deference to the British monarch. Some mountain men wrongly assumed the initials stood for the Green River in Wyoming, in whose valley their rendezvous were held. The confusion was understandable, for other knives they carried bore the name "Green River" on their blades. These, however, were made by the American firm of J. Russell at a factory on the Green River in Massachusetts. The mountain man's expression "up to Green River" was probably first applied in a literal sense to mean burying a knife "to the hilt" in an adversary's ribs. Metaphorically, it became a term of praise for any job done well.

The trade knife was an all-purpose tool whose uses were hardly limited to skinning, butchering, and self-defense. On many occasions it did yeoman service as a surgical instrument. A trade knife saved the life of trapper Tom Smith in a particularly grisly episode in 1827. During an Indian attack on his party, a bullet hit Smith just above an ankle, shattering the bone. In agony he cried out for someone to amputate his mangled leg. According to a contemporary account, after his companions balked at the gruesome task, Smith asked one of them for a knife, and with it "he severed the muscles at the fracture with his own hand." Another man then "took the knife . . . and completed the operation by severing the tendon achilles," then bound up the wound "with an old dirty shirt."

Tom Smith — thereafter known as Peg-Leg Smith — lost an extremity but gained a moniker, and the mountains gained another legend.

TODAY, ANYONE VENTURING into the wilderness would include among his gear a map and compass and probably a GPS device. Yet the mountain man and voyageur managed quite well with none of these aids. Of course, there were no maps to speak of other than the ones engraved on gray matter: it was said of Jim Bridger, who could neither read nor write, that he carried in his head a map of a third of the continent. After the fur trade ended in the 1840s, Bridger and other ex-trappers like Joe Walker and Kit Carson guided the army cartographers who produced the first detailed maps of the West. Walker's photographic memory of terrain dumbfounded the soldiers he led on an expedition in 1859. The old frontiersman took them up a part of the Colorado River he had gone down just once, more than twenty years before. Every morning prior to starting out, he drew an unfailingly accurate map of the country they expected to cover that day, showing where the valley widened and narrowed, where tributaries entered, and where they could find good grazing for their horses.

In *Across the Wide Missouri*, his magisterial tribute to the mountain man, Bernard DeVoto ponders the wilderness skills and exquisitely honed senses that enabled him to survive:

> Why do you follow the ridges into or out of unfamiliar country? What do you do for a companion who has collapsed from want of water while crossing a desert? How do you get meat when you find yourself without gunpowder in a country barren of game? What tribe of Indians made this trail, how many were in the band, what errand were they on, were they going to or coming back from it, how far from home were they, were their horses laden, how many horses did they have and why, how many squaws accompanied them, what mood were they in? Also, how old is the trail, where are those Indians now, and what does the product of these answers require of you? Prodigies of such sign-reading are recorded by impressed greenhorns, travelers, and army men, and the exercise of critical ref-

> erence and deduction which they exhibit would seem prodigious if it were not routine.

At the next level of insight is "the interpretation of observed circumstances too minute to be called sign.":

> A branch floats down a stream — is this natural, or the work of animals, or of Indians or trappers? Another branch or a bush or even a pebble is out of place — why? On the limits of the plain, blurred by heat mirage, or against the gloom of distant cottonwoods, or across an angle of sky between branches or where hill and mountain meet, there is a tenth of a second of what may have been movement — did men or animals make it, and, if animals, why? Buffalo are moving downwind, an elk is in an unlikely place or posture, too many magpies are hollering, a wolf's howl is off key — what does it mean?

"The mountain man" observed DeVoto, "had mastered his conditions — how well is apparent as soon as soldiers, goldseekers, or emigrants come into his country and suffer where he has lived comfortably and die where he has been in no danger."

FINALLY, AS THE ORDEAL OF Peg-Leg Smith makes plain, a mountain man's survival depended on sheer grit and the will to live. To last in a country where bears, Indians, or a simple miscalculation could kill him, he needed "the right stuff" (including luck) as surely as any astronaut. Bridger and Walker had it in spades. So too did Hugh Glass.

After a severe mauling by a grizzly while hunting in present-day South Dakota, Glass was tended by two companions for several days. When the trapper appeared near death, they left him to his fate. But Glass recovered enough to begin a hike back to Fort Kiowa on the Missouri River, 350 miles away. He had been stripped of his rifle and was so weak he covered most of the distance on his hands and knees. During one ten-day stretch he subsisted on cherries and buffalo berries, and later devoured raw the flesh of a buffalo calf after chasing off the wolves that had killed it.

Like most mountain men, Glass was known to embellish a tale, and a few historians dismiss his story as so much campfire talk. But none doubt the truthfulness of a similar account by Jim Clyman (the "surgeon" who repaired Jed Smith's lacerated head) telling of his 600-mile trek across much of present-day Wyoming and Nebraska.

Clyman had become separated from his party near South Pass. Indians had stolen his horse, and he started on his way back to civilization with only eleven balls for his rifle. Whenever he could after shooting a buffalo, he dug the spent bullet from its flesh and rounded it back into shape with his teeth. He killed three in a row this way, all with the same ball. Near the end of his journey game became scarce, but he happened upon two badgers fighting. When his rifle misfired, he grabbed a bone off the ground and clubbed them both to death. After gathering grass and willow bark, he sparked a fire using the flint from his rifle (Indians having also stolen his fire steel), then roasted the badgers and made moccasins from their hides.

That proved to be Clyman's last meal for a while. Weakened by hunger, and wet and cold from three days of unseasonable rain, he staggered on. After eighty days on the trail, he topped a rise and saw below him the winding Missouri and an army post with the stars and stripes waving over it. He literally fainted with joy.

Ten days later, the three other trappers in Clyman's party arrived at the fort "in a more pitible state if possible than myself," as he later described the scene. His companions, he learned, had lost all their bullets when crossing a river. No matter: they made new ones by stripping the brass mounting from one of their guns and pounding the metal into balls. The buffalo they killed with this makeshift ammo kept them going until they reached the fort. Like the hunter drinking from a buffalo's gut and the voyageur gagging down boiled lichen, they did what it took to survive.

6

Frank Forester: The Exile

On an October morning in the 1830s, three sportsmen — Tom Draw, Frank Forester, and Harry Archer — and their dogs set out on a horse-drawn wagon across the Hudson Highlands of New York. As befitting their time and station, they were dressed for the day's hunt in top hats, high-collared shirts with neckties, and tweed jackets with roomy pockets for priming caps and paper cartridges of powder and birdshot. For hunting in brambly cover they wore leather leggings that reached above the knee. Their destination was some wooded bottomland thick with woodcock.

Ordering the driver to stop, Harry slipped from the wagon and commenced loading his double-barreled fowling piece. He rammed a cartridge into the first barrel and was starting to load the second when a woodcock flushed from the roadside willows. With a swiftness that astonished his companions, he capped and cocked the loaded barrel, swung the piece to his shoulder, and, as the bird flashed across the road, dropped it with a perfect shot.

By now Tom and Frank were also loaded and ready. The dogs, a pair of setters, plunged into the thicket and began working ahead of the hunters. More cock flushed, and the woods rang with the report of their guns discharging nearly as one.

Sunlight cut through the drifting smoke, and the smell of black powder mixed with the aroma of earth and decaying leaves. It was a fine beginning to what would prove a memorable morning. By noon, when they broke for a picnic lunch of roasted woodcock, they'd bagged sixty-five birds.

The above scene comes from *The Warwick Woodlands*, a narrative of hunting in the lush hills and vales around the town of Warwick, New York, some forty miles northwest of Manhattan. The author was William Henry Herbert, an expatriate Englishman who, writing under the pen name Frank Forester, was America's first outdoor writer. His prodigious outpourings in popular journals like the *American Turf Register and Sporting Magazine* and a dozen books, including *My Shooting Box*, *The Deerstalkers*, and *Frank Forester's Fish and Fishing*, defined a sporting ethic and raised the national consciousness about conservation. He argued for stricter game laws at a time when Americans assumed there was no limit to the bounty of their woods and streams and bagging sixty-five woodcock was nothing special.

First published in 1845, *The Warwick Woodlands* was Herbert's most popular book. Following the literary conventions of his day, he wrote it and similar hunting idylls as pastoral, plotless fiction, whose main characters were often thinly disguised portraits of real people. "Tom Draw," for example, was modeled after Thomas Ward, the owner of the tavern where Herbert habitually stayed when he ventured to Warwick from his home in Newark, New Jersey. He painted Draw as a latter-day Falstaff — carrying an incredible four hundred pounds on a 5-foot-6 frame, a "mass of flesh" who yet could "walk his day from morn to sunset with the best of us." Herbert drew on parts of himself in creating both Frank Forester and Harry Archer. In *The Warwick Woodlands* the author Frank Forester portrays the character of the same name as an amiable fellow, happy to stay up half the night drinking and swapping stories with Tom Draw. But Harry Archer is presented as the consummate sportsman, with the best shooting eye and an instinctive knowledge of dogs and game.

Herbert's literary reputation rests on books like *The Warwick Woodlands*, but he also wrote romantic tales on subjects ranging from the heroes of ancient Rome to the wives of Henry VIII, translated French novels and Greek plays, and wrote poetry. He was a fine pen-and-ink artist, illustrating many of the nearly one hundred books that bear his name as author, editor, translator, or contributor. His career spanned an era when advances in printing technology and a rise in literacy made it possible for writers to make a living at their craft, but financial pressures affected the quality of his work. His contemporary Edgar Allen Poe said that Herbert had "written more trash than any man living," and he wasn't above repackaging his old works and palming them off on a publisher as new. He spent money — on guns, dogs, clothes, and binges in fancy hotels — as fast as he earned it. Herbert's chronic inability to manage his finances reflects a mercurial and difficult personality. He was a boozer and brawler, often overbearing, yet with a charisma recalling his spiritual kin Ernest Hemingway.

Along with his sporting narratives, Herbert wrote instructional treatises on hunting and fishing. The best of these is probably *The Complete Manual for Young Sportsmen*, published in 1856. These "how-to" works have aged better than the narratives and can still be read for both pleasure and practical advice. They make clear that Herbert possessed all the skills afield he attributed to his fictional alter ego Harry Archer.

He acquired many of those skills as a boy hunting snipe and partridge and riding to hounds on the moors of his native England, under the tutelage of his sportsman father, who, in his son's words, "always shot best when the shooting was hardest." Herbert Senior, the son of an earl and a man of independent means, was a former barrister and member of Parliament who had quit politics for a more contemplative life. After ordination in the Anglican Church, he had become the rector of Spofforth, in Yorkshire. When not hunting or ministering to his rural parishioners, he pursued his hobbies of botany and natural history; among his admirers was Charles Darwin, who named two species of plants in his honor.

The elder Herbert appears to have been patient with his son's

William Henry Herbert, the expatriate Englishman who went by the pen name Frank Forester, was America's first outdoor writer and an early proponent of conservation.

youthful failings. Young Harry, as he presumably was called, followed in his elder's footsteps to Eton and Cambridge, where he excelled in classical studies while piling up gambling debts that forced him to flee the country. The dean settled his son's accounts, though it meant liquidating part of the family estate, and he continued to help him financially after Harry's exile to America, in 1831. Herbert's biographer believes his banishment resulted from an act far worse than failure to pay his bills: some unknown but grave offense against "the rigorous social code of his class." Whatever the transgression, the man who became Frank Forester spent the remaining twenty-seven years of his life in the U.S. and never again set foot in England.

The twenty-four-year-old Herbert landed in New York and quickly gained a reputation for his flamboyant and volatile ways. He moved into a fashionable hotel, played the horses at a local track, and cut a colorful figure swaggering down Broadway in a brass-buttoned coat and knee-high Wellington boots jangling with enormous King Charles spurs. He was arrogant and at times insufferable, accusing his adopted country of cultural inferiority while touting his own aristocratic lineage. At his favorite watering hole, a tavern called Washington Hall, his jibes often led to fist fights. He once pulled a gun on a patron and shot at him but missed.

There was a gentler side to Herbert's personality. Within a few months of his arrival in the U.S. he took a position teaching Greek and Latin at The Reverend R. Townsend Huddart's Classical Institute, a boy's academy where he remained eight years, winning the respect and affection of scores of students. Excursions afield brought out his better nature, too. In the 1830s, most of Manhattan was still forest and farmland, with streams (now storm sewers) full of brook trout, and the wetlands of nearby Long Island and New Jersey teemed with waterfowl. Herbert made friends with wealthy young Americans who shared his love of sport; they introduced him to hunting in the Hudson Highlands and fly fishing in the Catskills for trout and in local bays for striped bass, bluefish, and weakfish.

Herbert's teaching job allowed him time to write romantic novels and freelance for magazines, but it wasn't until 1839, when a friend and fellow sportsman, William T. Porter, began publishing the *American Turf Register and Sporting Magazine,* that he began to see the value of writing about the outdoors. He had pegged his reputation on his romantic fiction, but his attitude changed after critics, some of whom had dismissed his novels as stilted knock-offs of Sir Walter Scott, heaped praise on his outdoor sketches.

Five years after pieces by Frank Forester began appearing in Porter's magazine, Herbert published them in book form as *The Warwick Woodlands*, subtitled "Things As They Were There, Ten Years Ago." This allusion to change became more explicit in later editions, after a railroad was built through the Hudson Highlands. What had once been a remote semiwilderness could now be reached from New York in a few hours for an excursion fare of fifty cents. Herbert railed against "the disgusting roar and screech of the steam engine" and the hordes of urban pot-hunters it carried. His beloved shooting grounds, he wrote, "now swarm on the first of July with guns more numerous than birds."

His lament echoes that of every sportsman who has seen his favorite hunting or fishing spot degraded by development or crowding. But it was also grounded in what Herbert saw as the obvious need to conserve the resource. Among other things, he advocated a closed season on woodcock until October so the birds could breed successfully. This and other suggestions (for example, restoring fisheries ruined by pollution and dams), although hardly radical, were ahead of their time.

Herbert's chief influence on the country's nascent conservation movement, however, was the message implicit in all his outdoor writing: that hunting and fishing have less to do with filling the belly than with nourishing the soul. After the Civil War, when sportsmen rallied to protect our natural resources from the ravages of industrialization, they chose as one of their patron saints the man they knew as Frank Forester.

In 1839, when Herbert was thirty-two, he went with another writer, Joseph Scoville, on a hunting trip to Maine. They stopped in Bangor to visit Scoville's fiancée, a pretty eighteen-year-old named Sarah Barker. In what must have been an awkward turn of events she jilted her betrothed for his dashing English friend. After marrying later that year, Herbert and his bride began a peripatetic existence, moving between Bangor, New York, Philadelphia, and Newark. They were frequently broke and at times must have lived in squalor. A son, Willie, was born in 1841, followed two years later by a daughter, Louisa. By then, Sarah had contracted tuberculosis. She died in March 1844, and cholera carried away Louisa four months later.

The bare facts of this double tragedy can scarcely convey the pain Herbert must have suffered. From far-off England, his father extended a hand. He established a trust to help his son financially and agreed to take on the responsibility of raising his grandson. Four-year-old Willie left for England to live with his grandfather and went on to a long career in the British Army. Herbert never saw him again.

Although modest, the trust enabled Herbert to purchase some land along the lower Passaic River, in New Jersey, and to build a house on it. He called his estate The Cedars. The property would later be swallowed up by the expanding city of Newark, but when Herbert moved there it was mainly woodland surrounded by orchards.

HERBERT'S OUTDOOR WRITING conveys a sense of the happy, enclosed world of a man in harmony with nature and himself. There is no hint of the writer's personal misfortune or the lonely struggle of his craft. In reality, the last fourteen years of Herbert's life were marked by increasing instability and despair. After his wife's death, he kept her portrait on a chair and gazed at it for hours at a time. He quarreled with publishers and cursed his solitary and often threadbare existence; during one particularly "wretched" Christmas, he complained, he was reduced to dining by himself on dried salt pork and stale bread. He mourned the passing of his old shooting pal Tom Ward (alias Tom Draw). The bright moments afield became fewer and farther between.

In the winter of 1858, he grasped again for some semblance of a stable life. At a theater in New York he met Adela Budlong, recently divorced from an actor (this in a day when both divorce and acting were less than respectable). Herbert was fifty years old and down at the heels, but he must have radiated a raffish charm. In a brief courtship Adela fell for him. Perhaps he hinted at his family's wealth without telling her that it was forever beyond his grasp. They married in Newark and retreated to The Cedars for their honeymoon, but one glance at her husband's seedy quarters brought home the terrible mistake she had made. Adela fled, sending divorce papers from Ohio.

Herbert was staying at a hotel in New York when he received the documents confirming his wife's desertion. Early in the morning of May 17, after hours in which he had swung between calm and hysteria in the company of Philip Anthon, one of his former students, he retreated to the bedroom and shot himself through the heart. To Anthon he uttered his dying words: "I told you I would do it."

In a farewell note, Herbert wrote that "of all lives, mine has been the most unhappy." Yet it was his zest for living and the joy he found in hunting and fishing that bursts from his writing, and for this he is remembered. Although he died a self-pitying recluse, he had lived an exuberant life as a sportsman, ranging the Warwick Woodlands in the cheerful company of friends, sharing his love of the outdoors and his concern that the wild land and the fish and game on which his enjoyment depended should be protected for generations to come.

7

John Muir in the Sierra

JOHN MUIR WAS A THIRTY-THREE-YEAR-OLD SAWMILL OPERATOR in Yosemite Valley in 1871, a year crucial to his development as a naturalist and conservationist: when Muir met Ralph Waldo Emerson, saw his first piece of writing published, and in the shadow of a mountain peak discovered a remnant glacier that would prove his controversial theory that ice had shaped Yosemite and its sister valleys of the Sierra Nevada.

The young Muir made a striking impression on anyone who met him. He was a sinewy figure of medium height, and with his long auburn locks, beard, piercing blue eyes, and tattered clothes he reminded many of a biblical prophet. The awesome backdrop of Yosemite, with its cleaved granite cliffs and spectacular falls, reinforced the image of a Jeremiah in his mountain retreat. Muir was not unconscious of this perception and occasionally thought of himself in similar terms. "Heaven knows," he wrote years later, "that John Baptist was not more eager to get all his fellow sinners into Jordan than I to baptize all of mine in the beauty of God's mountains."

His first view of Yosemite had come three years earlier, when the wanderlust that affected Muir all his adult life — his "good demon," a friend called it — brought him to the Sierra Nevada following a five-month, thousand-mile walk through the American South. In the Florida Keys he had nearly died of malaria but recovered sufficiently to travel to Cuba, a way station on a long-planned journey to South America. Steeped in the writings of the explorer-naturalist Alexander von Humboldt, Muir cherished a romantic dream of penetrating to the headwaters of the Amazon and descending it to the sea. Unable to find transportation, however, and reluctantly aware of the dangers of such a venture, he settled instead on California as an alternate destination — a fortunate decision for the future of conservation, as Muir was still weak from his bout with malaria and might well have perished in attempting to carry out his quixotic scheme.

He arrived by ship at San Francisco in March 1868 and immediately set out on foot for Yosemite Valley, 150 miles to the east. The peripatetic naturalist was unprepared for the splendor of a California spring. Gazing across the San Joaquin Valley, he saw it as "a vast level flower garden, smooth and yellow like a lake of gold," while the distant, snow-mantled Sierra appeared "so gloriously colored and so radiant, it seemed not clothed with light, but wholly composed of it, like the wall of some celestial city." The description is vintage Muir, even (in adverbial form) to the inclusion of his favorite and admittedly overused word, *glorious*. For all his effusiveness, Muir was curiously silent regarding his first glimpse of Yosemite several days later — perhaps, as his biographer Linnie Marsh Wolfe has suggested, because for once in his life he was struck dumb by what he saw.

Muir found work at the ranch of an Irishman named Pat Delaney, who sent him with a herd of sheep into the high country the following summer. Delaney was sympathetic to his herdsman's passion for natural history and packed along an assistant who could free him for occasional botanical and geological excursions.

In 1870, Muir hired on as a sawyer at the tourist house of James Hutchings. He would remain for the next four years in this wilderness cathedral, exploring his "Range of Light" and developing the glacial theories that — by pitting him against the redoubtable Josiah Dwight Whitney, one of the most eminent geologists of his day — would bring him to the attention of the outside world.

John Muir, from a photo taken in 1872, when he was 34, a year after his meeting with Emerson and his discovery that the snowfields of the Sierra plateau were in fact remnant glaciers.

THE NINETEENTH CENTURY WAS a golden era for natural science generally and geology in particular. The renowned Swiss naturalist Louis Agassiz had worked out the dynamics of alpine glaciers and showed conclusively that a great sheet of ice had once covered much of the northern hemisphere. As a student at the University of Wisconsin, Muir had read Agassiz and studied under one of his former pupils, Dr. Ezra S. Carr, and after leaving college he had spent three years in Canada exploring the glacial-gouged landscape north of the Great Lakes. Now, during his summer of shepherding, he noticed almost immediately that Yosemite's rocks were marked with ice striations. After further investigation he concluded that in the remote past a massive tongue of ice nearly a mile thick had advanced through the valley, shearing its granite walls and truncating the rounded summits of Half Dome and El Capitan.

Muir's deductions ran contrary to the prevailing notion advanced by Whitney, a formidable opponent. An 1839 graduate of Yale, he had participated in many of the pioneering state surveys of the pre–Civil War era and was a seasoned geologist by the time of his appointment as California's state geologist, in 1860. Over the next eight years he directed a team of brilliant young assistants in mapping much of the Sierra Nevada, all the while guarding the scientific integrity of his survey from the venalities of a legislature chiefly interested in learning where gold might be found.

Whitney's view of the Sierra Nevada was starkly at odds with Muir's. To Whitney, the landscape was not so much awe-inspiring as depressing. "The heights are bewildering," he wrote, "the distances overpowering, the stillness oppressive, and the utter barrenness and desolation indescribable." Yet, like Muir, he would one day champion the idea of making Yosemite a national park.

In 1865, Whitney accepted a professorship at Harvard while continuing as director of the California Survey. From Cambridge he brought his considerable intellect to bear on the origin of Yosemite. The valley's sheer cliffs and vertiginous, U-shaped profile resulted from a catastrophic collapse of the earth's surface "in the wreck of matter and the crash of worlds," as he described it in his *Yosemite Guide-Book* of 1869. While ice once covered much of the Sierra, Whitney wrote, its erosive effects had been minimal, and it had never entered Yosemite.

Mountain man Joe Walker probably glimpsed Yosemite from the Sierra plateau in 1833, although eighteen years passed before any white man entered the valley. By Muir's day it was hailed as one of the natural wonders of the world. Tourists from San Francisco hardy enough for the three-day trip via rail, stage, and horse usually arrived clutching Whitney's guide book. Thanks to Muir, as often as not they left persuaded that glaciation, not cataclysm, had been its shaping force.

James Hutchings, Muir's employer, had asked his sawmill operator to double as a tourist guide, and in his new role Muir relished the opportunity to explain his glacial theory. By 1870 Yosemite was drawing a thousand visitors a year. Some of these were people of influence, friends of Muir's old teacher at Wisconsin, Dr. Carr, who had lately moved to Oakland to join the faculty of the University of California. Ezra Carr and his wife, Jeanne, were great admirers of Muir, and they urged their friends to visit the valley and meet this brilliant if eccentric young man. News of Muir and his theory began to appear in newspapers, and eventually word drifted back to Whitney about the upstart amateur and his heretical ideas. The renowned geologist dismissed this interloper as "a mere sheepherder" and "ignoramus" whose "wild and absurd ideas" could never stand up to scientific scrutiny.

THE THIRD OF SEVEN CHILDREN and the eldest boy, Muir was born in 1838 in Dunbar, on the north coast of Scotland. He was eleven when his family emigrated to Wisconsin. His father, Daniel Muir, was a farmer and a rigid Calvinist who ruled the household with the severity of an Old Testament prophet. The elder Muir led the family in morning and evening devotionals, banned pictures as graven images, and forbade talking at meals out of respect for the Provider. He whipped his children for the mildest infractions and worked them almost literally to death. John recalled one harvest when he came down with mumps and was so sick he could barely stand "and sometimes fell headlong into the sheaves." Believing that "God and hard work" were the best cure, his father refused to let him see a doctor.

Ann Muir, his cheerful and unflappably pleasant mother, couldn't have been more different. The rest of the family seems to have inherited her unbreakable spirit, for they all conspired to have fun under the tyrant's nose. They made faces at the silent dinner table and danced jigs in the father's absence. Later, when the old man left home to minister to the poor in Hamilton, Ontario, they covered the walls with pictures and embroidery.

Nature and literature also provided escape from the drudgery of farm work. John Muir reveled in the wilderness surrounding his Wisconsin home; he read Shakespeare, Milton, and (unbeknownst to his father) lighter authors like Burns and Scott. Not unlike Lincoln thirty years earlier, he went to extraordinary lengths to acquire an education. From his arrival in America until his matriculation at the University of Wisconsin he had only two months of formal schooling. Using borrowed texts and employing the few hours between chores, he taught himself algebra, geometry, trigonometry, and shorthand.

Muir had a photographic memory and could cite verbatim long passages, including much of the Bible. In adolescence he showed a knack for invention that made him a legend in the community. He built an ingenious iron thermometer, a self-setting saw, and an "early rising machine" that at the designated hour tilted his bed and pitched him on the floor. Muir had a thing about clocks and carved them, gears and all, out of wood in the middle of the night, the only time available. One of his clocks was shaped like a scythe and in addition to time told the date and day of the week. Neighbors flocked to the Muir place to admire the prodigy's handiwork. Daniel Muir put a stop to his son's most ambitious project — a gigantic, four-faced Big Ben — saying it would draw too much attention to the farm. His real concern was his son succumbing to the sin of pride.

Muir was twenty-two when he broke free of the farm. He went to Madison to exhibit his inventions at the state fair, then stayed on to attend the recently established state university. He blossomed in his new environment — a classmate remembered him as "the most cheerful, happy-hearted man I ever knew." He was a top student and considered going on to medical school. Instead, he left the university before completing his undergraduate degree.

Muir claimed financial problems for dropping out, but the main reason was simple restlessness. Courses in botany and geology had awakened his incipient interest in natural history. While still a student he had made a lengthy field trip down the Wisconsin River into Iowa, writing adventure poetry along the way. Now more distant horizons — Canada, the deep South, and finally the Sierra Nevada — beckoned. "I was only leaving one University for another," he declared, "the Wisconsin University for the University of the Wilderness."

The five-year hiatus between Muir's departure from Madison and his arrival at Yosemite included a crucial incident that shaped his future as much as any single event. Going first to Canada (in part to avoid the Civil War draft), he worked as a mill hand and at other odd jobs, botanizing on the side and wrestling all the while with a basic conflict: whether to profit by his genius for invention or pursue his deeper interest in natural science. His quandary remained unresolved when, in 1866, he returned to the U.S. and went to work in a carriage-parts factory in Indianapolis. There, to his employer's delight, he began inventing machines to increase production. But an accident on the job one day left him blind in both eyes. Muir feared he might never see again. He swore if he recovered to bid "adieu to all my mechanical inventions" and devote himself to wilderness. Within a few months he had regained his sight.

While recuperating he chanced on an illustrated folder promoting the grandeur of a California valley called Yosemite. Until then his exclusive dream had been to see the Amazon. Now the great river would compete in his imagination with another, equally alluring natural wonder.

JANUARY 1871 FOUND MUIR snug for the winter in his "hang-nest," a small, boxlike appendage he had built onto Hutchings's sawmill. He could have lived in the nearby hotel but preferred the mill for its solitude, its "fresh piney smell," and the murmur of the Merced River running beneath his quarters. Muir had designed his nest with a sense of mountain aesthetics firmly in mind: twin skylights framed Sentinel Dome on one side and Yosemite Falls on the other, while the single window commanded a sweeping view down the valley.

Not even the harshness of a Sierra winter could deter him

from his forays into the high country. He made a week-long trek to the rim of Hetch Hetchy Valley, twelve miles north of Yosemite across the Tuolumne Divide, wading through snow five feet deep. As was his custom winter or summer, Muir lived on bread and tea or coffee and carried only a blanket. "I have been nearly blind since I crossed the snow," he wrote to Jeanne Carr on his return, more as a matter of fact than as a complaint. The professor's wife was trying to lure him back to civilization, but he obliquely declined her invitation to come live with the Carrs in Oakland: " 'The Spirit' has again led me into the wilderness, in opposition to all counter attractions, and I am once more in the glory of Yosemite."

Muir enjoyed playing to Jeanne Carr's maternal feelings in descriptions of his untethered life and the risks it entailed. In early April, several months after his wintry adventure on the Tuolumne Divide, he wrote her a midnight letter by campfire while perched, soaked and shivering, on a ledge by a waterfall, high above the valley floor. Muir had climbed to his aerie earlier in the day, intent on spending a mystical night in communion with the moon-spangled falls, and while squeezing onto a narrow shelf behind the falls had nearly been swept away. "I suppose I was in a trance, but I can positively say that I was in the body, for it is sorely battered and wetted."

WITH THE ARRIVAL OF SPRING it was time once more to pursue his glacial studies in the field. In two years of clambering about the landscape he had deciphered bits and pieces of the message left by the great ice sheets on the rocks. Now he hoped to put them all together in a coherent theory.

With spring, too, came the usual influx of tourists, including the most distinguished visitor to set foot in Yosemite to that time. Ralph Waldo Emerson's arrival came at the end of a transcontinental trip that had taken him to the Far West for the first time in his life. He was sixty-eight years old and America's preeminent man of letters. As the father of transcendentalism, Emerson basked in the light of his international reputation, but his intellectual powers had begun to fade. To Muir he would seem but the ghost of a great man, while the Boston literati who accompanied the aging philosopher worried over him like nursemaids.

Emerson and his party had come out from San Francisco, arriving in early May. Any skepticism he may have had about reports of the valley's sublimity vanished the instant he took in its towering walls and lush meadows. Yosemite, the old man declared, "is the only place that comes up to the brag about it, and exceeds it." Word quickly spread of the famous guest at Leidig's Hotel, and none of the valley's residents was more eager to make his acquaintance than Muir. "I was excited as I had never been excited before," he recalled years later. It was not until near the end of Emerson's stay, however, that Muir, "overcome by awe and reverence," screwed up his courage and sent Emerson a note "telling him that El Capitan and Tissiack [Half Dome] demanded him to stay longer."

Emerson had heard of Muir from Ezra Carr, and after receiving Muir's note he paid him a visit. The Brahmin and the mill hand hit it off at once. Muir invited Emerson and a companion, James B. Thayer, up the narrow ladder to the sanctuary of his hang-nest and once inside launched into a paean to his beloved high country while laying out his dried plants and pencil sketches for Emerson's inspection. Neither Muir nor Thayer, who functioned as Emerson's Boswell on his western trip, records any discussion about glaciers, but given Muir's obsession with the subject it must have come up in this or subsequent conversations. Obviously taken by this living ideal of the transcendental, who perhaps reminded him of his late friend Henry David Thoreau, Emerson spent much of the next few days in Muir's company.

A week after his arrival in Yosemite, Emerson and his entourage rode out of the valley and into the high country to see the Mariposa Grove of giant sequoias. Accompanying them was

Muir, who had accepted Emerson's invitation to join the group on condition that the old man promise to camp overnight under the canopy of big trees. Muir fairly gushed at the prospect: "I'll build a glorious camp-fire," he told Emerson, "and the great brown boles of the giant Sequoias will be most impressively lighted up, and the night will be glorious." At this, he recalled, Emerson "became enthusiastic like a boy, his sweet perennial smile became still deeper and sweeter, and he said, 'Yes, yes, we will camp out, camp out.' " Emerson's doting lieutenants, ever-protective of their venerable charge, would have other ideas.

The party of twelve, including several ladies, set out toward the grove, riding single file through the forest. Muir provided a running commentary while Emerson gazed in wonder at the towering sugar pines and Douglas firs.

At lunch the conversation, as it always did sooner or later in Emerson's company, reverted to literature. Earlier in his visit, standing before the majesty of Vernal Falls, one of his minions had quoted Longfellow's *Wreck of the Hesperus* while the old sage nodded approvingly. It seemed that every fresh experience evoked some poem or passage from Scott, Wordsworth, or Coleridge. Muir, whom Thayer noted was "not strong" on his literary points, bristled at their inability to appreciate the wilderness on its own terms.

Late in the day they arrived at Wawona and to Muir's everlasting disappointment decided to spend the night at the local hotel rather than push on the additional few miles to the Mariposa Grove. "It would never do to lie out in the night air," one of them said. "Mr. Emerson might take cold; and you know, Mr. Muir, that would be a dreadful thing." Muir protested — only "in homes and hotels" were colds caught, and in all the Sierra they would fail to find "a single cough or sneeze." But "the strange dread of pure night air could not be overcome. . . . Sad commentary on culture and the glorious transcendentalism."

The next day the group proceeded to the grove, and once again Muir tried to persuade the old man to sleep in the bower of the giant trees: "You are yourself a Sequoia. Stop to get acquainted with your big brethren." But Emerson was "past his prime, and was now a child in the hands of his affectionate but sadly civilized friends. . . . It was the afternoon of the day and the afternoon of his life, and his course was now westward down all the mountains into the sunset."

Muir elected to stay behind in the sun-streaked temple of the ancient trees. He watched as the party rode back toward civilization. As Muir remembered,

> Emerson lingered in the rear of the train, and when he reached the top of the ridge, after all the rest of the party were over and out of sight, he turned his horse, took off his hat and waved me a last goodbye. I felt lonely, so sure had I been that Emerson of all men would be the quickest to see the mountains and sing them. Gazing awhile on the spot where he vanished, I sauntered back into the heart of the grove, made a bed of sequoia plumes and ferns by the side of the stream, gathered a store of firewood, and then walked about until sundown. The birds, robins, thrushes, warblers, etc., that had kept out of sight, came about me, now that all was quiet, and made cheer. After sundown I built a great fire, and as usual had it all to myself. And though lonesome for the first time in these forests, I quickly took heart again — the trees had not gone to Boston, nor the birds; and as I sat by the fire, Emerson was still with me in spirit, though I never again saw him in the flesh.

After Emerson's death, eleven years later, the naturalist John Burroughs was going through his papers when he came upon a list with the words "My Men" across the top. Emerson had compiled it over the years. The last name, added in old age, was Muir's.

FOLLOWING HIS INTERLUDE with Emerson, Muir returned to his work at the sawmill. When he could find a free moment, he continued to guide visitors sent to him by the Carrs. Among these was Harry Edwards of San Francisco, a professional actor and amateur entomologist whose collections of butterflies and beetles were among the best in the world. Muir volunteered to collect for him and later that summer sent Edwards a box of butterflies, including two that were new to science.

But chasing butterflies amid the rocks and silver firs of the Sierra plateau was a mere diversion from the dominant task now at hand — a systematic exploration of every canyon and peak in the upper Merced watershed in a final assault at decoding what Muir called "the great open book" of Yosemite geology. The story of the valley's origin was written in the striations and moraines of ancient glaciers. He would read the rocks and weave their stories together into a coherent theory that in its mass of detail would refute Whitney once and for all.

Muir figured the job would take him several years. In early July, having saved enough money to live on for a while, he quit his job at the sawmill and set out with his duffle of bread and tea for six weeks' exploration in the high country. He returned in August just long enough to reprovision before taking off again.

He had his work cut out for him. In the valley the erosion of rain and frost had erased the direct evidence for glaciation. He reasoned that the record would be fresher at the higher elevations, where the glaciers would have lingered longer. To Jeanne Carr he wrote that Yosemite Valley was "the *end* of a grand chapter" whose beginnings would be found in the basins of high-country streams that spilled off the valley's cliffs. He was certain these basins had been carved by smaller glaciers that once connected to the big glacier that had carved Yosemite Valley.

As in the valley, much of the evidence for these smaller ice sheets had weathered away, but Muir became adept at finding striated rock in the protective shadows of glacial boulders. The grooves in these rocks revealed in what direction a glacier had flowed. Lateral moraines, eroded but still discernible to his practiced eye, indicated a glacier's width and depth. He told Jeanne Carr about comparing canyon with canyon, "with all their varieties of rock structure and cleavage, and the comparative size and slope of the glaciers and waters they contained. Waking and sleeping I have no rest. In dreams I read blurred sheets of glacial writing."

Although he had yet to publish a word on his glacial studies, Muir was becoming well known in geological circles. Two of the more august members of the scientific fraternity paid him a visit during that summer of 1871, Dr. Clinton L. Merriam of the Smithsonian Institution and John Daniel Runk le, president of the Massachusetts Institute of Technology. Merriam and Runkle came away convinced of the correctness of Muir's theories, and more importantly they convinced him to commit them to paper.

Others, including Emerson, had urged Muir to write, although he had always dismissed the idea — perhaps out of fear of rejection. It was now apparent that the scientific establishment was taking him seriously. After hiking for five days with Muir and seeing the evidence firsthand, Runkle told him he ought to write a book on his glacial theory and invited him to Cambridge to teach. Muir demurred on going east but promised him a manuscript in due course. Runkle agreed to send him scientific instruments to aid in his field work.

Muir eventually decided that his understanding of Sierra glaciation was far enough advanced to venture a short article on the subject, and sometime in early October he wrote a piece and mailed it to the New York *Herald Tribune*. To his surprise the editors accepted it, and on December 5 the story appeared near the back of the paper along with dispatches from Italy, Austria, and the Bahamas. It was titled simply "Yosemite Glaciers" and its unnamed author identified only as "an occasional correspondent of the Tribune."

Muir's first published writing began with an elegant conceit: "Two years ago, when picking flowers in the mountains back of Yosemite Valley, I found a book. It was blotted and storm-beaten; all of its outer pages were mealy and crumbly, the paper seeming to dissolve like the snow beneath which it had been buried; but many of the inner pages were well preserved, and though all were more or less stained and torn, whole chapters were easily readable. In just this condition is the great open book of Yosemite glaciers to-day."

In his closing section Muir described the "death" of the Yosemite Creek glacier and the pristine lake it had left in the shadow of Mount Hoffman, a major peak to the north of the valley. Muir assumed that all of the Sierra glaciers had long since passed into oblivion, but the mountains were about to prove him wrong.

AFTER MAILING HIS ARTICLE to the *Herald Tribune*, Muir set off for another exploratory jaunt, this time to the headwaters of Illilouette Creek to the east of Yosemite. With winter approaching it would be his last opportunity of the season for observation. "It was one of the golden days of the Sierra Indian summer, when the rich sunshine glorifies every landscape however rocky and cold, and suggests anything rather than glacier," he later wrote. Methodically he explored each of the river's tributary basins, examining their moraines and other glacial evidence while working his way up through a succession of vegetative zones. The firs and pines grew dwarfed as he ascended, finally giving way to alpine bryanthus and cassiope and arctic willows hugging the leeward slopes.

Climbing to the headwaters of Ottoway Creek, he camped for the night in a grove of mountain hemlock beside an alpine lake. The ring of mountains, he later wrote, formed a natural amphitheater crowned with the "crumbling spurs and battlements" of Red Peak to the north, a jagged ridge to the east, and Black Mountain to the south. On a bed of branches Muir slept the "clear, deathlike sleep of the tired mountaineer" and awoke the next morning ready for another day's exploring.

With sun streaming over the mountains, Muir followed the course of a creek linking a string of diminutive lakes like a pearl necklace. The last of these "lakelets" was little more than a widening of the creek, and on its bottom he noticed a covering of gray mud — "entirely mineral in composition, and fine as flour, like the mud of a fine-grit grindstone," material created from the grinding of glacial ice on rock. "Before I had time to reason, I said, 'Glacial mud — mountain meal!' "

Muir glanced ahead to the place where the creek trickled

from the base of a sloping, sixty-foot-high embankment of dirt and stone whose "raw, unsettled, plantless, new-born appearance" immediately suggested a glacial moraine of recent origin. He scurried to the top, stones cascading down behind him, and stood on the threshold of the greatest discovery of his life.

What at first glance appeared to be a huge snow bank sprawled before him, a half-mile wide, "swooping down from the gloomy precipices of Black Mountain." In its "stained and furrowed surface were stones and dirt like that of which the moraine was built. Dirt-stained lines curved across the snow-bank from side to side, and when I observed that these curved lines coincided with the curved moraine and that the stones and dirt were most abundant near the bottom, I shouted, *'A living glacier.'* "

Creeping along the edge of the glacier, Muir found crevasses whose luminous recesses revealed the laminated structure of the ice. Peering into one, he noticed how the snow grew more crystalline at greater depths until compressed into a kind of porous ice; finally, twenty or thirty feet down, it hardened into blue ice. Muir couldn't resist observing the marvelous structure close up. Carefully he made his way down between the glacier and the rocks

> into the weird underworld of the crevasse. Its chambered hollows were hung with a multitude of clustered icicles, amid which pale, subdued light pulsed and shimmered with indescribable loveliness. Water dripped and tinkled overhead, and from far below came strange, solemn murmurings from currents that were feeling their way through veins and fissures in the dark. The chambers of a glacier are perfectly enchanting, notwithstanding one feels out of place in their frosty beauty. I was soon cold in my shirt-sleeves, and the leaning wall threatened to engulf me; yet it was hard to leave the delicious music of the water and the lovely light.

Pressing eastward after his initial discovery, Muir climbed to the summits of Mounts Lyell and McClure, whose vast snowfield was also revealed as a vestigial glacier. The following summer he would hammer a line of stakes across the McClure glacier and return in the fall to find that the line had changed to a parabola, with the greatest movement near the center — proof, if more were needed, that these "snow fields" conformed to Agassiz's laws of glacial dynamics.

Muir continued his studies afield for the next two years, eventually discovering sixty-five glaciers. By 1874, having gathered enough data to write definitively on Sierra glaciation, he at last heeded Jeanne Carr's advice and came down from the mountains. Working at the Carrs' house in Oakland, he produced a series of articles for *Overland Monthly*.

Muir's findings secured his reputation as a scientist and gave him confidence to pursue his writing on natural history and conservation. His glacial investigations didn't end with the Sierra Nevada. In 1879 he made the first of four voyages to Alaska to probe the great ice-carved fjords of the Alexander Archipelago, one of whose glaciers now bears his name.

Besides Alaska, Muir's wanderlust took him in later years to the South Pacific, Asia, Africa, and — as an old man — to the Amazon he had longed to see since his youth. Although he settled down in his fashion to marry, raise a family, manage a successful orchard business, and work tirelessly for wilderness as the founder and first president of the Sierra Club, his "good demon" never deserted him.

8

The King of Diamonds

GEMSTONE FEVER SWEPT THROUGH SAN FRANCISCO LIKE A box-canyon fire. Stories circulated, growing grander with each telling throughout that giddy summer and early fall of 1872, about a "new Golconda" — a reference to the mythical city of Hindu riches — where diamonds, rubies, and other precious stones could be pried from the earth with a jackknife.

Rumors placed the bonanza on a mesa in Arizona or New Mexico, but the exact whereabouts remained the closely guarded secret of a company of California and East Coast investors. For $600,000 they had bought from prospectors Philip Arnold and John Slack all mineral rights to the fields. As proof of their fabulous find Arnold and Slack had a sackful of gemstones. Assays by a San Francisco jeweler and Tiffany's of New York confirmed that the stones, mostly diamonds, were genuine. The company's respected mining consultant, Henry Janin, inspected the fields and estimated their production value at a million dollars a month, on a par with the fabled Comstock Lode.

Stories of the gemstone jackpot piqued the curiosity of Clarence King, a flamboyant young geologist directing the United States Geological Survey of the Fortieth Parallel. Relying on the shards of information available from newspapers and their own intimate knowledge of western terrain, King and several of his survey colleagues deduced that the fields had to lie, not in the Southwest as rumored, but in the northwestern corner of Colo-

Clarence King in the field, ca. 1868. The celebrated geologist, mountaineer, raconteur, and bon vivant was hailed by his friend John Hay "the best and brightest man of his generation."

rado Territory, within the swath of the Fortieth Parallel survey. They determined to find them.

In October, late in the season and with snow threatening in the mountains, King and his team took the Central Pacific Railroad from San Francisco to Fort Bridger, Wyoming Territory, and hastily outfitted for a trek on horseback into the bleak country to the south. A five-day, 150-mile ride — at times in the teeth of subzero winds — brought them to a tabletop region of pine and sagebrush matching Janin's published descriptions. Mining claims posted along a narrow gulch bore Janin's name. Farther down the gulch King and his companions came upon a sandstone ledge where gritty soil bore weathered footprints. They dismounted and began to search. It took only a minute to find the first ruby, then another and another, then several diamonds.

Their excitement was tempered the following day. On closer inspection, King found everywhere the same twelve-to-one ratio of rubies to diamonds. Gems were plentiful in exposed areas but rare in hard-to-reach spots. He found combinations of stones that would never occur in nature and noticed that diamonds were concentrated at the soil's surface but absent at bedrock level, where their high specific gravity should cause them to settle. When King, as he later wrote, spied a diamond balanced on a rock "in a position from which one heavy wind or the storm of a single winter must inevitably dislodge it," the whiff of fraud became a stink.

King rode hard to the nearest rail station and boarded the first westbound train for San Francisco. Shares in the company had been scheduled to go on sale in a month, and his announcement that the fields were salted burst a nascent investment bubble and forestalled a possible financial panic.

The wealthy investors were innocent of this brazen fraud. A grand-jury investigation revealed they had been duped by Arnold and Slack, who had played their gambit with $35,000 worth of rough gemstones purchased in London several years before. By now the wily pair had fled beyond the reach of California law — Slack to St. Louis and Arnold, the scheme's mastermind, to Kentucky, where for a time he lived as a country squire on the take from his mighty flimflam.

KING'S ROLE IN EXPOSING THE FRAUD made him the toast of San Francisco and beyond — the story of what came to be called the Great Diamond Hoax was also front-page news in New York and London. He was lionized as "the King of Diamonds," a savior of the financial community and a paragon of science in the service of the people.

Although barely thirty years old, King had already come to the country's attention with a series of magazine articles about his adventures as a field geologist, first as a member of the California state survey led by Josiah D. Whitney, John Muir's antagonist in the debate over Yosemite's origins, and later as director of the federal survey of the Fortieth Parallel. In 1872 the articles were anthologized under the title *Mountaineering in the Sier-*

ra Nevada. Like Bret Harte's *The Luck of Roaring Camp and Other Stories* and Mark Twain's *Roughing It,* King's stories fed eastern readers' insatiable curiosity about the rough-and-ready life in California.

Mountaineering in the Sierra Nevada is a book only a young man could have written, bursting with an exuberance so appealing the reader forgives its lapses into the literary conventions of the day. (King had a fondness for the picturesque — "gloomy" deserts, "Dantesque" surroundings, and the like.) It intersperses his accounts of actual mountaineering with sketches of frontier types like the Newtys, a family of itinerant hog farmers with a wizened father and a tobacco-spitting mother. Their strapping daughter — "in the region of six feet tall, square-shouldered, of firm iron back and heavy mold of limb" — is the brawny prototype of a stock female in western fiction, capable of straddling a horse on the jump and kicking sense into the meanest razorback with her "cowhide eleven" boots. King greatly impresses the Newtys, even if the admiration isn't exactly mutual, and on his departure the old man hints that "half the hogs" are his should he return to take his daughter's hand.

In another chapter King describes outrunning two banditos bent on stealing the geologist's bulging gold-pouch. Riding a horse named Kaweah — "young, strong, fleet" and "fearfully wild, with a blaze of quick electric light" in his eye, King leads them in a breathless chase through the San Joaquin Valley and into the Sierra foothills. In quieter interludes he evokes the lazy ambiance of the long California autumn, when the hills grow sere and the very air "seems to ripen into a fascinating repose" that tempers even its desperadoes. Hidden in the brush while his pursuers ride past in the dark, King notes how one of them "broke out in a delicious melody, one of those passionate Spanish songs with a peculiar throbbing cadence, which he emphasized by sharply ringing his spurs."

King's romantic tale seems too good to be true, and in fact he may have created it out of whole cloth, for his official report for this period states that "nothing of interest" occurred. In a sly reference to his friend's penchant for embellishment or worse, Bret Harte inscribed a book to "Clarence King, author of Geology of the fortieth parallel and other works of fiction."

King was born in 1842 in Newport, Rhode Island, the first child of James King, a merchant in the China trade, and his sixteen-year-old wife, Florence. Two sisters followed, but both died in infancy. When King was six, his father died while on business overseas, leaving his widow to raise their sole surviving child as best she could. Florence doted on Clarence, home-schooling him in French, Latin, and Greek and indulging his interest in natural history as he turned their home into a veritable museum of rocks, plants, and fossils.

Florence King remained a dominant figure throughout her son's life. Two other influences were a loving black nursemaid and his maternal grandmother, Sophia Little, an abolitionist active in the underground railroad who imbued her grandson with an enduring respect for people of color.

King attended Yale's Sheffield Scientific School, where he excelled in chemistry, physics, and geology. His broader interests encompassed art, literature, and exploration. He reveled in Albert Bierstadt's vertiginous landscapes of the American West and devoured John Ruskin's rhapsodic essays about the Alps, as well as Washington Irving's history of the Rocky Mountain fur trade and John Charles Frémont's accounts of exploring Nevada and California.

The exposed flanks of western mountains were ideal for studying earth history, and King realized that working as a field geologist might offer him a way to fulfill both his scientific and literary goals. In the spring of 1863, a year after earning his degree, he headed west to join Whitney's California survey.

Crossing the plains with a wagon caravan, King could scarcely contain his enthusiasm for the wide, wild country that opened before him. In typical breakneck fashion he plunged his horse into a thundering herd of buffalo. A bull sideswiped King and his horse, throwing them to the ground. The impact killed the horse, but King walked away with a few bruises and a good story — the first of many that, told and retold around campfires and later in the salons of New York and London, would make him one of the era's most celebrated raconteurs.

During his first summer with the California survey King scaled Mount Lassen, in the Cascade Range, with Whitney's chief assistant, William H. Brewer, to trace old lava flows. On the descent he insisted on schussing down the snowy slope like a human toboggan, five hundred feet at a clip. From Lassen's summit, Brewer recalled, he burst into "rhapsodies of admiration" for the sweeping panorama dominated by neighboring Mount Shasta, glowing icy blue in the alpine morning. "What," exclaimed King, "would Ruskin have said if he'd seen *this!*"

King's reveries charmed Brewer, but the survey's senior paleontologist, the dour William Gabb, sized him up as one who "had rather sit on a peak all day, and stare at those snow-mountains than find a fossil in the metamorphic Sierra."

The assessment cut deep — King wondered if he had "really fallen to the level of a mere nature lover" — and caused him to rededicate himself to geology. Not long after, he proved his mettle by discovering, in a gulch called Hell's Hollow, a fossil squid establishing the geologic age of the Mariposa gold fields.

He still found time for mountaineering. Later that summer King and several colleagues made the first ascent of Mount Tyndall, and from its summit they glimpsed to the south a far grander peak. They were certain it had to be the tallest in the United States and named it Mount Whitney, after their boss. King vowed to climb it, but his attempt on the mountain later that summer failed several hundred feet short of the top. He swore to return.

In the winter of 1865 King and topographer James T. Gardiner were dispatched on temporary duty with the U.S. Army to map military roads through northern Arizona. The territory swarmed with Yavapai and Hualapai warriors itching for a fight.

One day, moving ahead of their cavalry escort, they found themselves surrounded by fifty Indians with drawn bows. Fearing the worst — torture and death — King and Gardiner in a desperate stall for time broke out their surveying instruments and put on an impromptu demonstration. Unimpressed, their captors ordered them to strip and began preparing a fire. In the best horse-opera fashion, the cavalry appeared in the nick of time and routed the Indians. The story of their hairbreadth escape became a favorite of King's in his growing repertoire of adventure tales.

King spent three years with the Whitney survey, acquiring the field expertise that led to his appointment, in 1867, as director of the U.S. Geological Survey of the Fortieth Parallel, the first of the pioneering national surveys for systematically mapping the West.

As envisioned by King, the survey would represent a hundred-mile-wide, west-to-east cross section of the continent. Running along the Fortieth Parallel from the Sierra Nevada to the Rockies, it roughly followed the line of the Central Pacific Railroad, then under construction. Using his connections from Yale and the California survey, on a trip to Washington, D.C., he gained a hearing with Secretary of War William Stanton, who endorsed the plan. A law was soon on the books creating the survey, with twenty-five-year-old Clarence King as its chief.

King wanted his scientific results to be on a par with those of the best European surveys, and without neglecting the practical matters of cartography and mining geology, he placed particular emphasis on discoveries that would advance basic science. He hired European-educated laboratory geologists whose application of chemistry and physics to the study of rocks led to a deeper understanding of the geological forces that had shaped the region.

Meanwhile, the conquest of Mount Whitney remained an obsession, and in June 1871 King again challenged the mountain that had beaten him seven years before. This time he reached the top — not of Mount Whitney, however, but of neighboring Mount Langley, some five hundred feet shorter. King failed to realize his mistake because swirling clouds hid the true Mount Witney from view.

King wrote a stirring account of his ascent, but his boast of being the first to reach "the summit of the United States" turned sour two years later, when another climber, the geologist Watson A. Goodyear, retraced King's route on a sky-blue day, with Mount Whitney plainly visible.

King was in New York when he got the news and left immediately for California. On September 19, 1873, he gained the summit of the true Mount Whitney. But he could no longer claim the honor of being first, for three parties had beaten him there in the preceding weeks. A month later, John Muir reached the summit and found an apologetic note from King explaining his error of two years earlier. "All honor," he wrote, "to those who came before me."

THE SEASON OF 1872 CLOSED OUT the Fortieth Parallel survey's active work in the field. For King it was a year best remembered for his exposure of the Great Diamond Hoax and publication of *Mountaineering in the Sierra Nevada.*

In the more mundane task of directing the Fortieth Parallel survey, King was gaining distinction within the scientific community. In 1870 the first in a series of detailed reports on the survey region appeared. Dealing with the survey's mining districts, it was followed by volumes on paleontology, petrology, and geography. The series's crowning achievement was *Systematic Geology.* Written by King and published in 1878, it detailed the author's comprehensive theory on the evolution of the basin-and-range system along the Fortieth Parallel. The massive, 800-page study laid out the geological history of a third of the continent and remained a standard reference well into the twentieth century.

In 1879 King was appointed first director of the newly created U.S. Geological Survey, charged with classifying all federal lands west of the Mississippi. But his enthusiasm for government service was waning. His $6,000 salary as director of the U.S.G.S. didn't come close to meeting his ambitions or his increasingly expensive lifestyle. Determined to capitalize on his knowledge of western terrain acquired during sixteen years in the field, he resigned his government post in 1880 and set out on a new phase of his life as an entrepreneur.

King had found fame and now he wanted fortune, but like Gatsby's beckoning green light it would remain forever beyond his grasp. Money for King was less an end in itself than a means for a life grounded in finer things. An inveterate if indiscriminate art collector, he aspired to be a great patron of the arts. More grandly, he aspired to make his life a work of art.

He launched into a series of mining ventures centered chiefly in Mexico, raising money among friends and directing operations from New York, where he took up permanent residence. None of the mines lived up to promise. By 1883 a need for more capital gave him an excuse for a European voyage to seek additional backers. He expected to spend only a few months away but tarried two years, succumbing easily to what a fellow expatriate called the "infectious orgy of idleness and frivolity."

Resplendent in a green velvet suit, King ambled through England and France and made a lazy tour of Spain, paying homage to Cervantes. In London and Paris he hobnobbed with the best bohemian society, talking till dawn about women and art, and charmed bankers and princes with his uproarious tales of western life. He met the intellectual hero of his youth, John Ruskin, who sold him the last two Turner paintings from his London home. Ruskin offered to sell him only one painting if he preferred, but King bought both. A compulsive punster, he quipped, "One good Turner deserves another."

Caught up in this glittering world, King spent a minimum of time on business and in the end failed to find new investors for the Mexican mines. His long absence without results exasperated his American stockholders, and they forced his resignation. It was King's first significant failure, but hardly his last.

THERE WERE OTHER SCHEMES to turn a fortune. In El Paso, Texas, King organized a bank that went under in the Panic of 1893. He had been living beyond his means for some time, and this latest disaster plunged him deeper into debt. He was already hopelessly in hock to a friend, the independently wealthy John Hay, who in the last years of King's life advanced him the equivalent in today's currency of more than $1 million. King never repaid a dime. Hay, ever sympathetic to his plight, never pressed.

As a young man Hay had served as Abraham Lincoln's White House secretary, and he would crown a distinguished diplomatic career as secretary of state in the administrations of William McKinley and Theodore Roosevelt. He was one of three close friends King could always count on. The others were James Gardiner, his old colleague from the California survey, and the historian Henry Adams, who would write poignantly of King in his classic memoir, *The Education of Henry Adams.*

Adding to King's money problems was a recent downturn in his mother's fortunes. Florence King had remarried when her son was in college and had two more children by her second husband. His recent death had left Florence and her family destitute and dependent on her first-born for support.

The personal and financial strain began to show. Usually immaculately dressed, King became disheveled. His memory lapsed. He suffered a nervous breakdown and was committed to an asylum. It was the low point of his life, yet King managed to keep his sense of humor concerning his "institution of learning" with its "open, frank lunatics." He was discharged after several months. Accompanied by Henry Adams, he sailed to Cuba for a three-month holiday that helped restore his spirits.

Despite his straightened finances King continued his memberships in a slew of social organizations befitting a man of his station. They included the Union League Club, the Downtown Club, the Tuxedo Club, the Metropolitan Club, and — his favorite — the Century Association, where he held forth night after night. In the words of biographer Thurman Wilkins, "The puns and quips, the jeweled phrases, the jokes and stories which fell from his lips were, evidently, legion; but as the Century had no Boswell, they were allowed to perish, leaving only a bright tradition."

ALTHOUGH KING HAD FLIRTED with the idea of marriage to a San Francisco girl while in his twenties, he remained a lifelong bachelor, at least in the public eye. In his mid-forties, however, he entered into a secret common-law marriage with Ada Copeland, a black woman eighteen years his junior. Ada worked in Manhattan as a nursemaid in a white household likely headed by an acquaintance of King's.

Henry Adams wrote of King's "dream of unfair women." King liked to tell his friends that "miscegenation was the hope of the white race" — a line tossed off as a joke, although he couldn't have been more serious. He was drawn irresistibly to Ada, who had been born a slave in Georgia in 1860. "Ah, my dearest," he wrote in one of his many moving letters to her, "I have lain in my bed and thought of you and felt my whole heart full of love for you. It seems to me often that no one ever love a woman as I do you. In my heart there is no place for any other woman and never will be."

He set up Ada in a house in Brooklyn, and later in Queens. She eventually bore him five children. Maintaining his double life, King continued to keep rooms in Manhattan, either at one of his clubs or in a residential hotel. He visited Ada between business trips, passing himself off to the neighbors as a Pullman porter, a job held exclusively by African Americans. In this parallel existence he went by the pseudonym James Todd. Ada also knew him as James Todd and believed his story about working for the railroad. They were married thirteen years. A few months before he died, King finally revealed to her his true identity.

To support his families (black and white) and his urbane lifestyle as a Manhattan clubman, King worked himself to exhaustion. In 1899, during an extended stay in Butte, Montana, on a mining consulting job, he contracted what was probably pneumonia. Tuberculosis followed, and his health rapidly declined. He journeyed to Phoenix, Arizona, for whatever relief the dry climate might afford his ravaged lungs.

Even near death he could flash his celebrated wit. Half comatose from a shot of medicinal heroin, he overheard the doctor remark that the dose may have gone to his head. Muttered King, "Very likely, many a *heroine* has gone to a better head than mine now." They were his last words. He died shortly afterward, on the day before Christmas, 1901, two weeks shy of his sixtieth birthday.

Near the end of his life King told James Gardiner about his marriage. After his death Gardiner told John Hay, who bought Ada a house in Brooklyn. For many years Hay, and later his heirs, paid her a monthly stipend. Hay also supported King's mother for the rest of her life. His generosity toward Ada came with the tacit understanding that she would keep her marriage to King a secret.

For years following her husband's death, Ada remained ignorant of her benefactor's identity. She believed the funds came from a trust King had left her, and in the 1930s she sued to get control of it. The trust did not exist, and the suit was dismissed. By going public, she forfeited future payments by Hay's heirs. She remained in the house Hay had purchased for her until her death, at age 103, in 1964.

John hay called king "the best and brightest man of his generation," unique "in his inexhaustible fund of wise and witty speech," in the way "his marvelous humor played like summer lightning over far horizons," and "above all in his astonishing power of diffusing happiness wherever he went." Henry Adams compared his charisma to that of Alcibiades and Alexander the Great, declaring, "One Clarence King only existed in the world." Praise of this sort spills into hyperbole, but it was typical of the encomiums lavished on the King of Diamonds by his Gilded Age peers.

In the end, King's dazzling personality outshone his accomplishments in science and literature: his greatest achievement was himself.

9

William Henry Jackson: Frontier Photographer

IN LATE JULY OF 1871 A PARTY OF THIRTY-FOUR MEN RODE UP THE valley of the Yellowstone River to its junction with the Gardiner River, near the southern border of Montana Territory. Leading the line of horses and pack mules was Ferdinand V. Hayden, director of the U.S. Geological Survey of the Territories — "the Doctor" to the men who had followed him during the previous five years in his pioneering surveys of the western lands.

Their destination was a strange and fabulous plateau of geysers and hot springs. Rumors of the upper Yellowstone's geothermal wonders had circulated for decades but had been widely dismissed as the tall tales of trappers and prospectors. The previous summer, however, an exploring party led by territorial officials Henry D. Washburn and Nathaniel P. Langford had confirmed the stories of boiling paint-pots and other fantastical features. The reports prompted Hayden to organize a more thorough expedition, one that would include field scientists like himself as well as an artist and three photographers to document the region's marvels.

Hayden, along with Washburn, Langford, and others, recognized the importance of preserving this unique landscape from haphazard settlement and exploitation. They were already talking about convincing Congress to set it aside as a national park. Time was of the essence, for gold had recently been found in the headwaters of the Clark Fork, a Yellowstone tributary, and soon the country would be overrun with miners.

On reaching the junction of the Gardiner River, an advance party that included photographer William Henry Jackson headed overland and came upon a sight to match the most mendacious of trapper tales. Jackson set up his dark-box, tripod, and bulky camera and after laboriously preparing a glass plate shot the first picture ever taken in Yellowstone: the scalloped terraces and reflecting brine pools of Mammoth Hot Springs, with the expedition's artist, Thomas Moran, standing in the foreground amid the mineralized steps.

The group pushed on, ascending Lava Creek and crossing the Yellowstone River on a ramshackle bridge built to accommodate the prospectors who had already begun trickling into the region. On a plateau overlooking Yellowstone Falls, Jackson encountered what he would call his "biggest photographic problem." The best place for photographing the falls, he realized, was not from the plateau but from the canyon two hundred feet below.

The dark-box in which the plates were prepared and developed, while nominally portable, was too heavy for the descent and had to remain on top. With the help of an assistant, Jackson unloaded the gear from his pack mule, set up the dark-box, and prepared a wet plate. Kneeling and inserting his head and hands in the holes of the light-proof calico hood, he balanced a glass plate on the thumb and fingers of one hand and poured a pool of collodion into a corner, then carefully worked the fluid over the surface. Next he immersed the plate in silver nitrate, whose light-sensitive salts formed in suspension with the tacky collodion film. The plate was backed with blotting paper to keep it moist, slipped into a light-proof holder, and the holder wrapped in a moist towel; the entire package was then placed in a dark-cloth.

With camera and tripod in one hand and plate in the other, Jackson scrambled down the steep sides of the canyon, set up the camera, made a fifteen-second exposure, and climbed back with

With the Grand Tetons in the background, William Henry Jackson prepares a wet-plate next to his dark-tent.

the exposed plate, reaching the top out of breath and in a wringing sweat. He developed the plate immediately, since the image would be lost if the collodion-nitrate solution had a chance to dry. Jackson made the round trip four or five more times. The end of the day found him "exhausted but very proud" of the results.

Given the primitive and cumbersome equipment of his day, the difficulties Jackson overcame shooting Tower Falls were typical of the problems he routinely faced in the field. ("Oh, that I had had a Kodak," he would lament years later.) He carried three cameras on the Yellowstone expedition: one 6½ by 8½ inches, another 8 by 10 inches, and a double-lensed stereoscopic for shooting the popular stereopticon pictures of his day. In addition there were tripods, trays, bottles, scales, and a supply of chemicals that included ten pounds of collodion, silver nitrate, alcohol, iron sulfate, potassium cyanide, and nitric acid, plus four hundred glass plates for making negatives.

The expedition's two other photographers, Joshua Crissman and Thomas Hines, found the conditions equally challenging.

After Crissman lost his only camera when a gust of wind blew it off a cliff, Jackson lent him one of his.

Ultimately, only Jackson's photos found their way into the portfolio of images Hayden showed government officials in his efforts to preserve Yellowstone; Crissman's pictures never circulated beyond Bozeman, Montana, and Hines's were lost in the Great Chicago Fire, two months after he took them.

Following Hayden's return to Washington, D.C., later that year, he joined with Langford and William H. Clagett, Montana's territorial representative, to lobby on Yellowstone's behalf. Their trump card was Jackson's prints. As Yellowstone's first historian, Hiram M. Chittenden, noted, "Description might exaggerate, but the camera told the truth; and in this case the truth was more remarkable than exaggeration."

On March 1, 1872, President Ulysses S. Grant signed legislation making Yellowstone the nation's, and the world's, first national park.

PHOTOGRAPHY WAS A "kind of inheritance" for Jackson, who was born in upstate New York in 1843 and as a child played with parts of a daguerreotype owned by his father. Quitting school at age fifteen, he worked briefly as a photo retoucher and scene painter before apprenticing himself to a photographer in Rutland, Vermont. The Civil War interrupted his fledgling career. After a two-year hitch in the army (he saw no combat but was part of a unit held in reserve at the Battle of Gettysburg), he returned to Vermont to resume life as a photographer's assistant.

Civilian routine proved agreeable. Jackson enjoyed his work, and his off-duty time was a constant round of picnics, tea dances, and poetry readings of Shakespeare and Longfellow. He was also courting the vivacious Caddie Eastman, a member of one of Rutland's best families. They expected to marry, but a minor disagreement burgeoned into a major quarrel, and they split. "She had spirit, I was bull-headed, and the quarrel grew," Jackson remembered in *Time Exposure*, an autobiography published in 1940. On the front porch she bid him an icy "Good night, Mr. Jackson." Bowing from the hip, he replied with equal formality, "Good night, Miss Eastman." After a week of misery he attempted a reconciliation, but the damage had been done.

Playing out his role in the tragicomedy, the twenty-three-year-old Jackson went into self-exile. With no particular purpose he boarded a train for New York City. There his fortunes plunged further when a pickpocket relieved him of his wallet and he was forced to pawn his watch for cash. Things began to look up when he ran into a couple of old army pals with an itch to scratch — they were bent on bumming their way west, and Jackson was eager to join them. The three had enough money for train tickets as far as Detroit, where they survived "near starvation" working odd jobs for two months before continuing on to Nebraska City and hiring out as teamsters on the Oregon Trail.

In their plug hats and paper collars, Jackson and his friends drew the "profanely pointed comments" of veteran bullwhackers, but their lack of experience scarcely mattered. They learned on the job, driving their twelve-ox teams with rawhide whips up the Platte and Sweetwater rivers through Devil's Gate and South Pass. At Ham's Fork, Jackson braved the wagon master's wrath and quit to join a party of Mormons on their way to Salt Lake City.

His adventures were typical of thousands of young men pouring into the West in the booming post-war era. From the Great Salt Lake he wandered to Los Angeles, then up to the Sierra goldfields for a try at prospecting, eventually signing on as a drover herding two hundred half-wild horses from California to the railhead at Julesburg, Wyoming. From there he continued on to Omaha and with his pay purchased a shave and a haircut and a fresh suit of clothes.

Jackson was tired of the footloose life, at least for a while, and decided to settle down as a photographer. He established a commercial studio, and his brother Edward soon joined him in the business. Omaha was a bustling railroad town and Jackson had as much trade as he could handle. He varied the routine of wedding parties and shop openings with visits to nearby Indian reservations to photograph members of the Pawnee and Omaha tribes.

Eventually he went farther afield to photograph construction on the Union Pacific Railroad, then nearing its rendezvous with the Central Pacific line at Promontory Point, Utah. While away from his studio he experimented with making prints in the field. The routine called for floating a sheet of albumen paper in silver nitrate, fuming it with ammonia, then laying the negative on top of the paper in bright sunlight. Once he had an exposed image the paper was washed, toned, fixed, dried, trimmed, and mounted. Success elated him, but often as not the process failed. He was still learning on the job.

Jackson would have been at Promontory Point to record the historic link-up, but it happened on the same date — May 10, 1869 — as his wedding to Mollie Green of Warren, Ohio. They had met when she was visiting relatives in Omaha. Three years later Mollie died in childbirth, along with their infant daughter. In his autobiography published sixty-eight years later, Jackson dealt with the tragedy in a few brief sentences: "These are matters about which, even now, I can write no more."

Ferdinand Vandeveer Hayden, professor of geology at the University of Pennsylvania and since 1867 chief surveyor for the Department of the Interior, stopped by Jackson's studio in July 1870. The two men had met briefly the previous year when Jackson was photographing near Cheyenne. Hayden was interested in obtaining some of the pictures he had taken of the Green River formations, but after examining them and remarking on their striking detail, the geologist asked the photographer to join him on his expedition that summer. Jackson instantly accepted.

He was generally familiar with the territory Hayden had planned to survey, since part of it lay along the Oregon and Mormon trails and the Union Pacific line. Leaving his studio business in disarray, he joined the survey in Cheyenne. In early August the twenty-man party began its journey up the Platte and through South Pass into the Green River country and the Wind River and Uinta ranges. Jackson's camera framed the spectacular Flaming Gorge, where John Wesley Powell had passed the previous year on his pioneering descent of the Green and Colorado rivers. At a Shoshone encampment near Camp Stambaugh, on the Continental Divide, he photographed Washakie, the tribe's legendary chief, in front of his lodge. This and others of Jackson's approximately two thousand Indian plates later formed the core of the photographic collection of the U.S. Bureau of Ethnology.

In total, Jackson's cameras and other photographic equipment and supplies weighed some three hundred pounds. This prodigious load was packed on the back of mules, animals whose vagaries he came to know all too well in his seven years as Hayden's chief photographer. He wrote lovingly and loathingly of the "fat little" Hypo, short for hyposulfite of soda, a fixing agent (1870, western Wyoming); the "evil" Gimlet (1872, Grand Tetons); Old Maggie (1873, Colorado Rockies); "little crop-eared Mexico" (1874, San Juan peaks and Mesa Verde); and Blinky (1875, Pueblo villages). Mules were the bane of the Hayden expeditions — charging into rivers to protest their loads, miring themselves in mud, and rampaging out of control down the streets of frontier towns. Yet as Jackson also noted, they were "indispensable collaborators" in surveying the West, able to work all day on scant water and forage.

The 1870 survey gave Jackson important added experience in field photography, under the most demanding conditions he had yet faced. Despite the difficulties of working from pack mules over rugged terrain, he found he could prepare, expose, and develop up to seventeen plates a day, "something of a record for wet-plate work." He learned to improvise — on a Uinta Peak he caught and melted snow in a rubber blanket for use in his developing solutions. All this was unbeatable training for the 1871 Yellowstone expedition.

The Hayden survey returned to Yellowstone in 1872, extending its work into the park's southwest quadrant. In 1873 it moved south to Colorado, in part to avoid troubles brewing in Montana and Wyoming with the Lakota Sioux. For the first time Jackson's photographic unit was designated a separate division and spent the early part of the summer shooting the high-country splendors along the Front Range, from Estes Park down to Pikes Peak and the Garden of the Gods. Jackson spent much of his time above fourteen thousand feet. Since mules balked at ascending such heights, the photographer and his assistants would backpack their equipment the last few thousand feet to the summit. Despite unusually inclement weather and a minor disaster when the "vagrant" Gimlet slipped his pack and broke a box of negatives, Jackson captured spectacular vistas amid some of the highest mountains in the contiguous United States.

His triumphs that season also included the first photos of the fabled Mount of the Holy Cross. For years prospectors had reported an unusual sight at the northern end of the Sawatch Range: a mountain bearing the outline of a perfect cross formed by snow-filled crevasses along its flank. The cross had been glimpsed on occasion from Grays Peak, forty miles distant, but on closer approach seemed to vanish like a mirage. After several days of hard climbing, Jackson reached a point where he could photograph the elusive mountain. Three years later, his prints won medals at the Philadelphia Centennial Exposition and inspired Henry Wadsworth Longfellow to write a popular poem, *The Cross of Snow*.

Before departing for field work, Jackson became engaged to Emilie Painter, a woman he had met through her father, an Indian agent on a reservation near Omaha. He and Emilie married in October 1873 and went on to have three children.

The survey of 1874 brought Jackson back to Colorado, through Estes, Middle, and South parks to the San Juan peaks, in the southwest part of the territory. Once again he had his own photographic unit, although for expediency he limited the size of his cameras to 5 by 8 inches. In Cochetopa Pass he photographed a band of Utes under Ouray, a highly regarded chief whose willingness to pose convinced others to stand for portraits. The sessions ended abruptly when Jackson erred in photographing a younger chief's infant and his camera was declared bad luck.

Jackson shot alpine lakes and valleys rimmed by snowy peaks; his camera framed the Rio Grande winding amid the cliffs of Wagon Wheel Gap and the boom town of Silverton sprawling at the foot of Sultan Mountain. Late in the season he ventured into the canyon country of the Four Corners to capture the ancient cliff dwellings of Mesa Verde.

JACKSON LEARNED OF the abandoned cliff towns from an old Omaha acquaintance, E. H. Cooper, a miner who by chance passed through Jackson's camp in September. Cooper was working at a placer mine along the Plata River. Not from there, he said, were "cliff dwellings and other ruins more wonderful than any yet discovered." The man to guide them was John Moss, chief of the mining camp and "high muck-a-muck" of all the La Plata region. Ernest Ingersoll, a newspaperman accompanying the photographic unit, was also eager to see the cliff houses and report them to the outside world. Jackson and Ingersoll were soon on their way down the Animas Valley toward the placer digs.

Moss rode out to meet them and agreed to act as guide. He knew the semidesert country north of the San Juan as well as anyone and enjoyed the trust of the southern Utes, who left his camp alone while harassing other whites in the region. Moss took the survey team into parched Mancos Canyon, where they found old mounds and pottery shards along the trail but, by day's end, none of the expected cliff houses. Jackson wrote in his diary that he was feeling "a little doubtful & discouraged."

When they pressed Moss as to the exact whereabouts of the

dwellings, he grinned and swept his hand across the rim of the 800-foot-high cliffs looming above them, a gesture underscoring the remoteness of the ruins and the difficulty of reaching them. So, when a sharp-eyed packer scanned the rock walls and announced he saw what looked like a house, it came as a surprise to everyone — especially Moss, who knew only of cliff dwellings deeper in the canyon. Jackson recalled how "closer inspection of the dusky shadows . . . revealed the square lines and small dots indicating a house with windows, sandwiched between layers of sandstone far up the canyon walls."

Although night was approaching and there would be no opportunities to photograph until the next day, the group scrambled up the talus at the base of the cliff for a closer look. A nearly vertical wall faced them the last fifty feet of the climb, and while the others elected to go no farther, Jackson and Ingersoll pushed on. Using a log as a makeshift ladder and finding some hand- and foot-holds probably made by the cliff dwellers themselves, they worked their way up to the shallow cave sheltering the ancient house, "perched away in a crevice," Jackson observed, "like a swallow's or bat's nest."

The little house was only about twelve feet high, its rooms divided by sandstone partitions with reddish plastered walls. A wooden floor separated the first and second levels. Today it is known as the Two-Story House and is part of Mesa Verde National Park. Over the next several days Jackson and his party explored and photographed more of the area, finding additional evidence of the culture that had died out so mysteriously five hundred years before.

Jackson returned to the Four Corners in 1875 with William Henry Holmes, an archaeologist and future chief of the U.S. Bureau of Ethnology. They visited Pueblo villages and explored more of Mesa Verde as well as ruins at Canyon de Chelly, Sierra Abajo, and Sierra La Sal. The stark, sun-drenched landscape captivated Jackson, and of all parts of the West this became his favorite. To do it justice he included among his equipment that year a gigantic 20-by-24-inch camera, nearly twice the size of any he had taken into the field before. Its larger negatives provided the finest resolution he had ever obtained. With this bulky leviathan Jackson also rephotographed many of the scenes shot the year before in the Colorado Rockies.

In 1876 Jackson took a season off from field work to represent the survey at the Centennial Exposition in Philadelphia; his photographs and a scale model he had made of the Mesa Verde cliff dwellings were star attractions. Hayden's plans for 1877 called for a return to Wyoming and Montana, but Jackson made special arrangements to tour the Presbyterian missions among the Hopi and Navajo pueblos west of Santa Fe. Having put up for years with the ponderous and time-consuming wet-plate method, he decided to experiment with a new, highly touted dry film from England. He ordered enough for four hundred 8-by-10-inch exposures, but at the end of the season, when the film was processed, Jackson found to his dismay that he had waited too long to develop the film, and it had failed to hold the exposures.

What Jackson called a "short, uneventful" 1878 season in Wyoming closed out the Hayden decade in the West. The following year, Congress merged the various territorial surveys into the new U.S. Geological Survey, under the direction of Clarence King. No longer on the government payroll and with a growing family to support, Jackson moved to Denver and set up where he had left off nine years earlier, as a commercial photographer.

Once again he found work with the railroads, which were eager to promote tourism by publicizing the West through scenic photographs. Over the next two decades most of the major western lines found use for Jackson's skills. His horizons expanded in 1894 when he embarked on a sixteen-month, globe-girdling junket as official photographer for a private commission inspecting railroads around the world.

In 1898 Jackson moved to Detroit to work for a company turning out color reproductions with a new photolithographic process, eventually becoming plant manager. By now he was semiretired from field work. His wife, Emilie, died in 1917, and seven years later, at age eighty-one, he retired for good — or so he thought — when the business went into receivership. Unable to collect some $6,000 due him in back pay, he got by on his Civil War pension and moved in with his daughter's family in Washington.

In many respects life began anew for Jackson in his eighties. He seemed ageless, dividing his time between writing and painting in winter and revisiting his old haunts in the West each summer — now carrying a "vest-pocket" Kodak. On speaking tours around the country he found audiences eager to hear his firsthand tales of the Old West. "It has all been very pleasant, this business of growing old," he wrote. He thrived in the out-of-doors, camping in the open while fending off efforts to coddle him. On one outing he rebuffed a well-meaning attempt by fellow hikers to include a cot for him. A blanket roll and the ground, Jackson insisted, was all he had ever needed.

At age eighty-five he had the good fortune to meet Ezra Meeker, a feisty nonagenarian thirteen years his senior. As a young man in 1851 Meeker had made the Oregon Trail crossing, and he later founded the Oregon Trail Memorial Association. "Uncle Ezra" took an immediate liking to the photographer — perhaps, Jackson speculated, because "he preferred to deal with a 'seasoned' man instead of with the whippersnappers of sixty or seventy who surrounded him" — and hired him as the association's research secretary, a position he held for the rest of his life. This arrangement entailed a move to New York, where he settled in at the Explorers Club as resident artist and raconteur. To New Yorkers he became known as the sprightly old soldier who marched down Riverside Drive each Memorial Day with the dwindling band of Civil War veterans.

Neatly dressed in jacket and tie, with gold-rimmed glasses and white hair, moustache and goatee, Jackson was a revered and legendary figure when he toured Grand Teton National ark on horseback at its dedication, in 1929. He was eighty-six by then and continued riding until age ninety-four, when he fell through an open cellar door in Cheyenne, Wyoming, landing on concrete ten feet below and breaking four vertebrae. After a month in bed he was up and about again, and except for a slight stoop was none the worse for the accident.

Jackson attributed his longevity to heredity — his father lived well past eighty and his mother to ninety-one — and to an active nature. "I have been too busy doing interesting things and getting ready to do even more interesting things," he explained in *Time Exposure*, published when he was ninety-seven. "As for drink, I am guided by the title of a recent book which, although I have not yet had time to read it, sounds very sensible to me. It is called *Liquor, the Servant of Man.*"

As a living link to a historic past, Jackson was often in demand for ceremonies of one sort or another. In 1935 he helped mark the seventy-fifth anniversary of the Pony Express, celebrated by three hundred Boy Scouts riding relays between Sacramento, California, and Saint Joseph, Missouri, and was aboard the plane that carried the message the rest of the way to Washington for delivery to President Franklin D. Roosevelt. Three years later, along with six thousand other members of the Grand Army of the Republic and three thousand Confederate veterans, he mustered at the seventy-fifth anniversary of the Battle of Gettysburg. Jackson and three others paid tribute to their long-dead comrades-in-arms by flying over the battlefield and strewing the cemetery with roses.

Although he never forsook the camera, in his later years Jackson turned increasingly to paintbrush and palette to satisfy his creative instincts. When he was ninety-two the Interior Department commissioned him to paint four large murals commemorating the early days of the Geological Survey. He later executed other paintings for the National Park Service and a series of watercolors recording the history of the Oregon Trail.

Jackson's last painting was, appropriately, a sunset over Laramie Peak in Wyoming, a region he had first glimpsed while driving his ox team toward South Pass three-quarters of a century before. His son, Clarence, later recalled, "My father was just one month past his 99th anniversary when I watched him finish this little masterpiece. Presently he put away his paints and brushes and leaned back for a final survey of his work. Then he sighed gently and said, almost in a whisper, *'There, it's done.'*"

Not long afterward the old man fell in his room at the Hotel Latham. The ensuing illness was brief. Jackson died June 30, 1942, and two days later was laid to rest with military honors in Arlington National Cemetery. His legacy lives on in fifty-four thousand images of the American West, fixed in silver nitrate on glass.

10

Custer Goes Hunting

ON THE PLAINS OF KANSAS ON AN APRIL MORNING IN 1867, George Armstrong Custer went looking for sport. Posted to the frontier only a few months before, the twenty-seven-year-old commander of the Seventh Cavalry was new to this stark landscape and eager to test his riding and shooting skills against its game. Astride a thoroughbred and escorted by a pack of hunting dogs that were his constant companions in the field, he galloped off from the column to run some antelope.

The fleet pronghorns soon left hunter and hounds in the dust, but on a nearby bluff Custer spied a buffalo and another chase was on. Horse and bison thundered neck and neck over the rolling prairie, just a few yards apart. His blood up and yelling like a Comanche, Custer cocked the hammer of his Colt and took aim. He was about to shoot when the buffalo veered and closed on the horse and rider. Custer grabbed at the reins to control his mount — and by accident pulled the trigger. The Colt exploded in a flash of fire and smoke and sent a bullet into the horse's brain.

The thoroughbred dropped like a stone and Custer went flying. He later admitted that the incident "came very near costing me my life," but the golden-locked cavalryman survived with all but his dignity intact. He might have broken his neck in the fall, or been gored to death, but instead the buffalo gave him a beady-eyed glance and sauntered off.

Custer was lost and horseless in Indian territory and miles from his command, which no prudent officer would have left in the first place.

With no real sense of direction he started walking. Within an hour he saw a cloud of dust on the horizon — sure sign of horsemen, but whether Indians or soldiers he had no idea. Through field glasses he watched a column come into view. As he later described it, he then "caught sight of an object which, high above the heads of the approaching riders, told me in unmistakable terms that friends were approaching. It was the cavalry guidon, and never was the sight of stars and stripes more welcome."

The misadventure was typical of Custer's luck and reckless physical courage — attributes that during the Civil War had worked for him as the Union's dashing "boy general" (at twenty-four, he had been the youngest brigadier in army history) and that, for a time at least, would continue working for him as an Indian fighter. The Great Plains would be home to Custer for most of the remaining nine years of his life. Between now and his disastrous defeat at the Little Big Horn in 1876 he would spend more time chasing game than pursuing Sioux and Cheyenne.

In those years following the Civil War railroads had begun to penetrate the prairies. Sodbusters and cow towns followed in their wake, but most of the vast grasslands between the Missouri and the Rockies were still the hunter's paradise that Lewis and Clark had known sixty years before. For a cavalryman of that time and place, hunting helped make tolerable an otherwise mean and hardscrabble existence. It was an antidote to the boredom of camp routine and provided the mess with fresh game to leaven a diet of salt pork and hardtack. Hunting was also training — running buffalo, which Custer likened to the "wild, maddening, glorious excitement" of a cavalry charge, challenged his courage and horsemanship, and taking a bead on an elk or pronghorn at five hundred yards sharpened his shooting eye.

For officers especially, hunting was part of a martial lifestyle as old as the profession of arms. The ambitious Custer used it to further his career and cultivate his cavalier image. He wrote about his exploits in the sporting press and organized buffalo hunts for visiting V.I.P.s, inviting reporters along to cover the spectacle.

People who knew Custer either loved or hated him, and few figures in American history have remained more controversial. To his legions of detractors, then and now, he was an egotistical glory hunter — rash, immature, narcissistic, irresponsible — whose misjudgments led directly to the debacle on the Little Big Horn and the loss of 268 lives, his own included. Custer was once court-marshaled and suspended from duty for abandoning his command in the field to return to his wife, whom he desperately missed. (Libbie Custer and her beloved "Autie" had a passionate relationship, and as a widow she defended him fiercely for fifty-seven years, until her death at age ninety, in 1933.) In official reports Custer wasn't above altering facts to vindicate himself and place blame for his failures on others, and in his hunting tales he was prone to exaggeration. Whether he lied or merely embellished depended on one's view of him: an army friend said Custer didn't distort the truth so much as magnify it.

In many ways Custer, who was just thirty-six years old when Crazy Horse and his Oglala warriors cut him down on Last Stand Hill, never grew up, but retained throughout his life the energy and headlong enthusiasm of an eight-year-old. He could ride hard from dawn to dusk, then stay up most of the night writing hunting stories and letters to Libbie which could run to 120 pages overflowing with wonder about the world around him. He reveled in the sweep and austere beauty of the plains, a landscape other army men saw as tedious and threatening. Endlessly curious about its wildlife, he kept a menagerie that at various times included a pronghorn calf, a porcupine, a burrowing owl, a badger, a black bear, and a pelican.

Most of all Custer loved hunting on the plains, and as the army's most colorful and charismatic officer he was the natural

Custer poses with a grizzly killed on the Black Hills expedition in 1874. Others in the picture are Bloody Knife, his Arikara scout, and Private John Noonan and Captain William Ludlow. The grizzly took bullets from all four men, and while Custer claimed the kill, Bloody Knife probably fired the fatal shot. Two years later, Bloody Knife died with Custer at the Little Big Horn.

choice to host a hunt arranged for a Russian royal son touring the United States. Staged on the prairies west of Omaha in 1872, the two-day shoot was an extravagant affair supplied with wagonloads of champagne and caviar and escorted by cavalry and infantry, with a band of friendly Brulé Sioux adding a touch of the exotic. At the center of it all was the Grand Duke Alexis, an affable twenty-one-year-old with muttonchop whiskers and a lust to kill a buffalo from horseback — a feat he accomplished on the first morning with coaching from Buffalo Bill Cody, the flamboyant and self-aggrandizing professional hunter and scout, who for the occasion lent the duke his best horse and gun.

After killing the buffalo Alexis jumped to the ground, then whacked off its tail with a knife and held the dripping trophy aloft, howling like a steppe wolf.

When Alexis expressed doubts about an Indian's ability to down a buffalo with a bow and arrow, Custer arranged for a demonstration: a mounted Brulé chased one into camp and before the duke's astonished eyes sent an arrow clean through it. That night the Sioux danced before a blazing campfire while the white hunters feasted on buffalo, elk, deer, antelope, turkey, duck, and prairie dog.

On a second hunt, held a week later in Colorado, Custer put on a bravura performance, using only his knees to turn his horse at full gallop while firing his pistol both right- and left-handed. "You ride like a Cossack!" exclaimed the admiring royal — the highest praise he could give.

Approaching a buffalo herd, Custer and Alexis were leading a party of soldiers, civilians, and Custer's boss, the volatile General Phil Sheridan. When Custer got it in his head to show Alexis how the army fought Indians, he ordered his troopers to attack the herd like they would a band of hostiles. Alexis and Custer led the charge, blasting away with their six-shooters and unleashing mayhem as everyone joined in the fray. (All but Sheridan. With bullets flying he threw himself to the ground in choleric rage, cursing the blood-lusting damnable duke.)

When the shooting stopped, Alexis bounded from his horse. He smothered Custer in a bear hug and planted a fat kiss on his cheek, then counted his kill: a dozen buffalo, which were promptly butchered and placed on ice for shipment home to St. Petersburg.

The year following Alexis's hunt found Custer operating

on the northern plains out of Fort Abraham Lincoln, in Dakota Territory. The Seventh Cavalry spent the summer in the vanguard of a 1,900-man force protecting survey crews plotting the course of the Northern Pacific Railroad. General Alfred Terry, the regional commander, predicted the expedition would be a "big picnic," and so it proved.

Except for a couple of skirmishes, the Indians mostly left them alone. Custer had ample opportunity to hunt, both for sport and to keep the expedition supplied with meat. He led hunting parties almost daily, and game was so plentiful they seldom ventured out of sight of the wagon trains. In a letter to Libbie written after a month in the field, he boasted, "I have done some the most remarkable shooting . . . and it is admitted to be such by all." His bag to date: forty-one antelope, four buffalo, four elk, seven deer, two wolves, and a fox, plus geese, ducks, prairie chickens, and sage hens "without number."

A taxidermist on the expedition taught his craft to Custer, who took to it with his usual zeal. As reported to Libbie, "I can take the head and neck of an antelope, fresh from the body, and in two hours have it fully ready for preservation." He was especially proud of the job he did on the carcass of a huge bull elk he pursued with his greyhounds. After Custer wounded the elk, the dogs ran it into the Yellowstone River. Custer watched from shore as they tore into it, anxious that one or more of his canine corps might be killed. A second shot finished the elk for good.

The greyhound that led the charge was probably Custer's favorite, a bitch named Tuck. In one of his endless letters to Libbie he asked, "Did I tell you of her catching a full-grown antelope-buck, and pulling her down after a run of over a mile?"

Tuck was one of some forty hunting dogs Custer owned at this point in his life, and he treated them all like members of his extended family. Back home at Fort Lincoln they had the run of the Custers' big frame house — tracking mud on the floors, leaving prints on the bedspread, stealing and wolfing down meat intended for the Custer table. Libbie tolerated her home being turned into a kennel and her husband's penchant for sleeping with his dogs: "I have seen them stretched at his back and curled around his head, while the nose and paws of one rested on his breast." A visitor recalled Custer's hounds following their master wherever he went on the post: on the spur of the moment he would throw himself to the ground and instantly come to resemble "a human island, entirely surrounded by crowding, panting dogs." When one of his favorites died in a hunting accident, Custer was moved to compose an elegy to "Poor Maida, in life the finest friend / The first to welcome, foremost to defend." On occasion he took his dogs into battle — one of them was killed in his controversial attack on a Cheyenne village on the Washita River, in Oklahoma, and another may have survived the Little Big Horn.

Custer killed his trophy elk with a new 50-caliber Remington rolling-block sporting rifle; that and a 50/70 Springfield were his weapons of choice for long-range shooting. After every successful shot he paced off the distance and carefully recorded it. His longest took down "a fine buck antelope" at 630 yards, and he claimed an average distance exceeding 250 yards.

He was vain about his marksmanship and in his copious writings never mentioned those occasions when someone outshot him. George Bird Grinnell, a naturalist on the Seventh Cavalry's 1874 expedition to the Black Hills, recalled an impromptu shooting contest between Custer and Luther North, Grinnell's assistant and an accomplished scout and hunter. Grinnell and North were riding with Custer ahead of the command one day when they came upon some unfledged ducks swimming on a kettle pond. Custer slid from his horse and announced, "I will knock the heads off a few of them." As Grinnell told the story,

> I looked to Luther North and made a sign to him and he dismounted and sat down on the ground behind the general. General Custer fired at a bird and missed it and North shot and cut the head off one of the birds. Custer shot again and missed and North cut the head off another bird. Custer looked around at him and then shot again and again missed and North cut the head off a third duck.

At that point an officer galloped over the hill and saved Custer's face by informing him the bullets were skipping off the pond and over the heads of his troopers. "We had better stop shooting," Custer said, and remounted and rode on without another word.

Grinnell also thought Custer overrated his greyhounds, "which he told everyone had overtaken and killed many antelope. They did nothing of this kind on the Black Hills expedition, and, though they chased antelope frequently, they never caught any. They did kill plenty of jack rabbits."

It was in the Black Hills that Custer, as he put it in another letter to Libbie, "reached the hunter's highest round of fame" by shooting his first (and only) grizzly. He took credit for the kill, even though the bear was also shot by three others in the hunting party. Bloody Knife, his trusted Arikara scout, probably fired the fatal bullet.

Bloody Knife had an easy relationship with Custer, and if he felt any resentment he kept it to himself. At other times he enjoyed tweaking Yellow Hair about his marksmanship, telling him he couldn't hit a tent from the inside.

CUSTER'S EXPEDITION to the Black Hills was notable for the discovery of gold. The Lakota rightfully claimed that the government had ceded them the Black Hills. When miners rushed into the region they went on the warpath, setting the stage for the campaign that brought Custer to his denouement at the Little Big Horn.

In June 1876 the Seventh Cavalry spearheaded a coordinated effort that attempted to trap the Indians on their hunting grounds in south-central Montana. While the Seventh approached from the east and another force advanced from the north, 1,250 troopers led by General George Crook moved up from Fort Fetterman, in Wyoming. Then, just eight days before Custer's fateful encounter, the Lakota stunned Crook in a fight on the Rosebud River.

The Indians killed twenty-eight soldiers and wounded fifty-six. Crook still had well over a thousand men, and he could have sent the wounded back to Fort Fetterman with an escort and continued north with the bulk of his force. He did send the wounded back, but instead of pressing on he withdrew to his base camp in the Big Horn Mountains, near the headwaters of the Tongue River, and waited for fresh supplies. Had he stuck to the plan he might well have hooked up with Custer, and history would surely have been different.

Crook was a brave soldier and one of the army's ablest Indian fighters, and his inaction has long puzzled historians. But the reason for it may be simple. He was never enthusiastic about this campaign, and after their mauling on the Rosebud he decided to treat his troops and himself to some R&R. The country teemed with game, and Crook loved to hunt almost as much as Custer. He was also an enthusiastic angler, as were many of his officers and men, and the Tongue and its tributaries were choked with trout. One of the general's aides likened the journal he kept to "the chronicle of a sporting club," its pages filled with accounts of stupendous catches — up to five hundred fish a day and many "thousands of fine fish taken" over the course of a two-week idyll.

So Crook and his men went fishing and hunting, while Custer plunged on toward destiny.

11

The Last Buffalo Hunt

ON THE RANGE THE HIDE HUNTER'S ROUTINE SELDOM VARIED. Rising at dawn, he shook off the Dakota cold, then joined the rest of the outfit for a breakfast of bacon, sourdough bread, and coffee. There was no need to hurry — give the buffalo time to eat their fill. That way, many of them would be at rest when the killing started.

The October sun had burned off most of the frost by the time he set out, carrying about forty pounds of gear, including a .45-caliber Sharps rifle, a hundred cartridges in two belts slung across his shoulders, and a leather scabbard containing a honing steel and a pair of knives for ripping and skinning. He worked alone and usually on foot, a stealthy approach being easier without a horse. As he neared the top of a rise, he dropped to his knees and elbows and crawled into position to view the herd spread out below him. About 10,000 buffalo, he guessed, were scattered in small groups across the undulant prairie. In the distance he could hear the familiar boom of Sharps from the other outfits working on this bright, Indian summer morning of 1883.

In the draw below him, a group of about fifty animals fed contentedly on the yellow grass. With the barrel of the big Sharps propped on a weathered buffalo skull, he estimated the distance at 150 yards. Selecting an old cow on the periphery of the herd, he took aim behind the shoulder and squeezed off a shot. He wanted to immobilize the cow with a lung shot to keep it from running off and stampeding the herd. The buffalo shuddered on the bullet's impact but stayed standing. When blood began pumping from its nostrils the hunter knew he had shot true. It dropped to the ground. The legs quivered, then were still.

Some of the others in the herd looked up at the report, and when one of them moved toward the fallen cow he took aim at his second target. For the next hour he picked them off one by one. Finally, he hit a young bull in the leg. He fired again and managed to down it as it limped away, but the rest of the herd was now alert to danger and began moving out of range. He might have pursued but elected not to. Several dozen dead buffalo lay in the short grass, and it would take the better part of the day to skin them out.

There was a rhythm to skinning that took him about ten minutes per animal: Heave the carcass over and wrench the head against the shoulder as a chock to hold it. With the ripping knife, girdle the legs and make a long incision from chin to tail. Pare back the hide with the skinning knife, jerk it free from beneath the carcass, and spread it out on the grass to dry, inside up.

They would return in several days with a wagon to collect the hides. A few years before, when the herds had numbered in the hundreds of thousands, a hunter could work out of a single camp for months, and the hides might be left out on the range for most of the season. But a herd of this size could be wiped out in a matter of weeks. Moreover, this herd was on the move, pushed east by the relentless shooting toward the Lakota reservations along the Grand and Moreau rivers, and the hunters would have to move with it.

In the decades following the Civil War, the numbers of professional buffalo hunters plying their bloody trade on the western prairies grew to many thousands. Buffalo had been killed in great numbers earlier by such men, but the coming of railroads like the Kansas Pacific and the Atchison, Topeka and Santa

In October of 1883, Sitting Bull led his Lakota warriors off the Standing Rock Reservation to hunt buffalo for one last time.

Fe provided an efficient way of transporting buffalo hides east. Once the rails had penetrated the plains, the slaughter began in earnest.

In the early 1870s the southern prairies had still been so thick with buffalo as to defy description. Each spring, massed in herds that might be twenty miles wide and sixty miles deep, they followed the ripening grasses north, moving out of Texas and the Indian Territory and into the phalanx of hunters spread across western Kansas into Colorado. At the height of the killing as many as 20,000 hunters may have been waiting for them. The hunters generally took only the hide, leaving the carcass, which on an old bull might weigh 1,500 pounds, to rot.

Mountains of pressed buffalo robes, meanwhile, crowded the freight docks of towns like Dodge City and Wichita. A good hunter could average 60 buffalo a day and might kill 3,000 in a single season. In the wake of the hunters came others to gather up the bleached bones, which were stacked by the railroad tracks in piles up to a half mile long, to be carried east for crushing into fertilizer.

By 1879 the southern herds were gone — vanished, in a wink of time, from a landscape they had dominated since the end of the ice age, 10,000 years before. The hunters shrugged in disbelief at their own bloody efficiency, then moved into the remaining buffalo country north of the Platte River.

Railroads opened up the Montana and Dakota ranges to wholesale slaughter, just as they had in the south. When the Northern Pacific pushed up the Yellowstone River in 1881, the towns of Glendive and Miles City sprang into existence as centers for the northern hunt. A typical hunter working out of Miles City might have one partner and two additional hunters, each hired at $50 a month. His outfit would consist of a pair of wagons and eight draft horses, two saddle horses, two tents, a field stove, three Sharps rifles, and enough powder, lead, primers, shells, knives, and provisions to last from October to February, the season of the buffalo's winter pelage.

An outfit's expenses might total $2,000, but with the price of buffalo robes averaging $2.50 apiece and with a kill of at least 6,000 animals, an outfit might make, in a good year, $13,000 in profits — a return on investment of better than 600 percent.

The first two years of concentrated hunting on the northern range were good indeed, but by the end of the third year the herds were vastly shrunken. The accounts of one New York jobber reflected this decline: He bought 26,000 robes and hides in the spring of 1881 and 45,000 in 1882; following the 1882-83 season, he shipped only 7,500. Hunters also noticed this precipitous drop, but many chose to ignore it. What about the estimated 75,000 head seen crossing the Yellowstone on its way toward Canada just that spring? This immense herd would return, they were certain, to supply the trade at least through another year. And so in the fall of 1883 the buffalo hunters prepared as usual for another season in the field.

PREOCCUPIED BY THE KILLING, the hunters didn't notice the tiny figures crouched on buttes to the east. Under the high October sky, Lakota scouts listened to the distant pop of rifles carried on the wind and watched the herd drift slowly in their direction. It had been less than a fortnight since the hunt had started, but already the herd had shrunk by nearly half. Still, the appearance now of even 5,000 buffalo was a source of wonder and astonishment — vindication, perhaps, of Sitting Bull's prophesy that *Pte*, the buffalo, would return and that the white men would vanish from their land.

The Lakota Sioux had depended on the buffalo for as long as they could remember. It was their standing crop, sustaining them with food, clothing, and shelter. Meat from the succulent hump ribs filled their bellies in summer. Dried, mixed with berries, and pounded into pemmican, it carried them through the snow months. Buffalo chips fueled their lodge fires. The dressed hides of buffalo covered their tipis and were fashioned by squaws into moccasins and leggins. Untreated, a fresh buffalo skin was impervious to water and could be made into kettles or stretched on a willow frame to create a bullboat. The matted wool of a buffalo robe was their mattress and winter blanket. The thick hide from a bull's neck, hardened with glue boiled from the hooves, made a war shield tough enough to turn an arrow. They used braided hair for rope and sinew for bowstrings. Ribs became knives and sled runners. From buffalo horn — boiled until supple, then cut into strips and bound together with rawhide — they crafted bows that could send an arrow clean through a bull.

The people responsible for controlling Indians recognized the buffalo's central importance to the Lakota and other plains tribes. A few conservationists were expressing concern about the slaughter, and in 1874 Congress debated the matter. The Secretary of Interior said he favored killing off the buffalo as a way to subdue the Indians once and for all. A bill to protect the buffalo passed anyway but died when President Grant refused to sign it. The following year the Texas legislature considered a similar bill and was advised by the regional military commander, General Phil Sheridan, that each hide hunter ought to receive a medal: "Let them kill, skin, and sell until the buffalo is exterminated, as it is the only way to bring lasting peace and allow civilization to advance."

Nor were the Indians flawless conservationists. But given their relatively small numbers, primitive weapons, and fondness for running buffalo on horseback — a more sporting and exciting, if vastly less efficient, way of hunting them — Indians made little dent in the bison population. Blame for the buffalo's demise lay squarely with the *Wasichus*, or white eyes, overrunning their country.

For a while, the Lakota had succeeded in stemming the flow of whites through their land. Red Cloud, perhaps their greatest chief, in 1867 had soundly defeated the U.S. Army, closing off the Bozeman Trail through their hunting grounds along the Powder River. But eight years later the discovery of gold in the Black Hills brought a new invasion and fresh conflict, culminating in Custer's debacle at the Little Big Horn.

Of all the Lakota leaders, none fought longer or more fiercely to preserve the old ways than Sitting Bull, the victor at Little Big Horn. After the battle he had retreated with his followers into Canada. But settlers had done as thorough a job of killing off the buffalo there as they had in the south, and game was scarce. Sitting Bull's people grew hungry and weary of exile. So in the summer of 1881 he led them back across the border and surrendered at Fort Buford, on the Missouri.

The army held Sitting Bull prisoner for two years before releasing him to the Standing Rock Reservation, where white officials hoped he would take up farming and become a model for the rest of the Lakota. (He refused.) Soon after, in an act of cruel if naive irony, officers of the Northern Pacific invited him to speak at the dedication of their new railroad, whose construction had been directly responsible for the decimation of the buffalo on the northern plains. Accompanied by an army interpreter, the most famous Indian in North America arrived at Bismarck and delivered a scorching diatribe in his native Lakota. "I hate the white people," he told the assembled. "You are all thieves and liars. You have taken away our land and made us outcasts." In place of these remarks, the interpreter substituted friendly platitudes. The crowd gave Sitting Bull a standing ovation.

SITTING BULL WENT HOME to Standing Rock, where the Lakota were reduced to living on government handouts of beef and flour. The army also delivered cattle on the hoof to the reservation, but rather than slaughtering these animals conventionally, the Indians ran them on horseback, killing them with bow and arrow or with the few ancient trade guns the soldiers had allowed them to keep.

Longhorns were a sorry substitute for buffalo, so in October of 1883, when the Lakota got word of a large herd approaching from the west, it seemed too good to be true.

In June of the previous year, a herd of comparable size had appeared near the western border of the reservation. The Standing Rock agent, James McLaughlin, ordered rifles issued to the Indians and accompanied them on that hunt. McLaughlin described these events years later but made no mention of an 1883 hunt, which suggests that Sitting Bull and the thousand warriors who accompanied him to meet the herd did so without agency permission.

A brief record of the 1883 hunt is preserved in an account by William T. Hornaday, a naturalist and chief taxidermist at the Smithsonian Institution, who interviewed several white market hunters who took part in the killing. (Hornaday would become a tireless campaigner in the buffalo's behalf and play an important role in rescuing the animal from extinction.) Although no first-hand Lakota account of the 1883 hunt exists, descriptions of earlier ones allow us to imagine it in all its ritual and anticipation.

Once safely removed from agency headquarters, the hunters set up camp. Beyond the circle of lodges they collected in two crescent-shaped lines laid out on an east-west axis, the crescents joined at the east end and open at the west. Sitting Bull sat along the south crescent with other elders, in front of a painted stone, a kind of altar. A half-dozen scouts — an elite group selected for their hunting abilities and moral character, whose task was to ride out in advance to determine the herd's size — gathered around the stone and swore to Sitting Bull to report correctly on what they saw. The old headman sealed the oath by drawing on a pipe, then touching the earth with it and raising it to the sky in tribute to *Wakan Tanka*, the Great Spirit, and to the buffalo god *Tatanka*. Each scout took the pipe in his turn and repeated Sitting Bull's gestures.

The ceremony over, the scouts headed out on their ponies. Some of the others escorted them a ways. They were all in high spirits, whooping and yelling and forgetting for a moment the humiliation of agency life and the likelihood that the buffalo they would soon encounter might be the last they would ever see. After a few miles the escorts broke away and raced back to camp. As the lead rider passed the painted rock he aimed his mount at three freshly cut bushes lined up about ten yards apart, knocking them down like ducks in a row — a sure augury of the hunt's success.

The hunters set out early the next morning and before long met the scouts returning with their report. The herd, which in early summer had numbered an estimated 10,000, was dwindling fast, and by the time the Lakotas were upon it and had joined the white hunters in the fray it was down to perhaps 1,200 head — scarcely one per warrior. It took the Lakotas just two days to finish them off in a final, furious melee.

As the hunters prepared the meat for winter, the old man who had led them watched and ruminated. The historian Mari Sandoz pictures Sitting Bull in his lodge,

> his pipe cold beside him, remembering the great Indian and buffalo country he was born into. It was just over on the Grand River there, the year before the fire boat, the Yellowstone, came smoking up the Mis-

> souri. Now all of it was gone, vanished like wind on the buffalo grass. True, he had known glory, much glory, but his broad face was hard as the walls of the upper Yellowstone when he thought about it, for what is glory to a man who must see his people as he saw them now.

In their own camps, the white hunters talked about what they had seen. No lovers of Indians, they had felt nonetheless an unexpected sympathy for the Lakota in what was certainly their last buffalo hunt. There were more buffalo out there, they told themselves, but they were west of here and far out of range of the Indians confined to their Dakota reservations. The hide hunters would not realize for another month that the buffalo they were talking about had been obliterated along the Canadian border by other white hunters and by half-starved Blackfeet and Assiniboines. The only survivors were a few strays that took refuge in the Missouri Breaks. Three years later, William Hornaday would scour these remote badlands and turn up 275 head, nearly half of all the buffalo left on earth.

Thanks largely to the efforts of Hornaday and other conservationists, buffalo would make a slow but steady comeback, from an estimated 635 in 1886 to perhaps 80,000 today — an impressive number, yet insignificant compared to the 40 million that once may have roamed North America. The great herds were gone forever, and with them any hope for a return to the old ways. Sitting Bull spoke for the Lakota and all the plains tribes in his song:

A warrior
I have been. Now
it is all over.
A hard time I have.

12

Out West with T.R.

The sun had dipped below the mountain, and the light was fading fast when Theodore Roosevelt, a thirty-one-year-old gentleman sportsman and rancher, topped a ridge on the Continental Divide in Wyoming and spied the dark, humped form of a grizzly. The bear was sixty yards off, upwind and moving away — it neither smelled nor saw him. Without hesitating Roosevelt raised his Winchester rifle and fired into its flank. As the shot echoed off the mountain, the bear grunted and plunged downhill into a laurel thicket.

Showing the reckless courage that would one day make him famous, Roosevelt raced down the slope in pursuit. With rifle ready, he skirted the edge of the laurels, squinting from behind wire-rimmed spectacles, trying to glimpse his wounded quarry. He could hear the bear growling in pain — "a peculiar, savage kind of whine," he later recalled — but the twisted branches hid it from view.

Suddenly, at a point where the thicket narrowed and thinned, the grizzly emerged from the brush. Raised up on its hind legs, the bear rolled its great head, seeking its tormentor's smell in the cold air. The bear was close enough for the hunter, despite the gathering dusk, to glimpse bloody foam around its mouth. He raised his rifle and fired again.

As the second bullet hit home, the bear roared, then wheeled and charged. Roosevelt squeezed off a third shot that hit square in the chest, but the bear kept coming.

The grizzly's swiftness and ability to absorb punishment astonished Roosevelt, but he held his ground, and as the bear closed he got off a final shot that smashed its jaw. He leapt out of the way as the grizzly hurtled past, then jammed more cartridges into the Winchester's spent magazine, but there would be no need to fire again. Examining the carcass, he noted with satisfaction that each of his first three shots had inflicted mortal wounds.

Roosevelt would ship the bear's skin back east to Sagamore Hill, his estate on Long Island, New York, where through the long damp winters it would evoke memories of his beloved West and the bracing freedom he enjoyed there.

By the fall of 1889, when the grizzly incident took place, Roosevelt had been coming West for six years and had bagged at least one of every big-game animal found beyond the Mississippi. Of all the game he pursued, none got his adrenalin pumping faster than the grizzly. Its ferocity when wounded made it the most dangerous quarry in North America; and as Roosevelt declared in one of several books he wrote on western hunting, although "danger ought never to be needlessly incurred, it is yet true that the keenest zest in sport comes from its presence, and from the consequent exercise of the qualities necessary to overcome it."

Chief among those qualities were coolness, intelligence, and physical courage — all of which the future president possessed in spades. He believed the good hunter must also be "persevering, watchful, hardy, and with good judgment; and a little dash and energy at the proper time often help him immensely." At the bottom of his list of attributes was marksmanship. Stalking and steadiness were a lot more important, Roosevelt asserted, for "if a man is close it is easy enough for him to shoot straight if he does not lose his head."

Roosevelt was notoriously near-sighted, so his emphasis on getting close to his quarry was understandable. The future president regarded himself as "only an ordinary shot," but a careful

Theodore Roosevelt posed in full hunting regalia — including a knife from Tiffany — in a New York City studio in 1885, when he was 27. Perhaps out of vanity, he removed his glasses; without them he was nearly blind.

reading of his hunting exploits suggests that even this assessment might be generous.

Teddy roosevelt's love of hunting grew out of a childhood obsession with natural history. His wealthy father, a patriarch of one of New York City's oldest families, presented twelve-year-old Teedie, as he called him, with his first rifle, for collecting animal skins. (To the boy's frustration, his marksmanship was hopeless until he acquired a pair of glasses.) As a bespectacled adolescent he roamed the fields and marshes of Long Island and New Jersey, shooting upland birds and waterfowl. Later, during summer vacations from Harvard, he hunted in Maine for moose and caribou. But hunting in the East — even for such larger game as could be found in the North Woods — paled in comparison to the sport that awaited him in the West.

Roosevelt came of age in the years following the Civil War, a period that saw the West transformed. What had been a wild, unbroken country roamed by Indians and teeming with wildlife

— most notably the vast herds of buffalo — had become, by the time of Roosevelt's first trip beyond the Missouri, in the summer of 1883, a region crisscrossed by railroads, with the tribes confined to reservations and the game rapidly disappearing. Buffalo, which a scant few years before had numbered in the tens of millions, were all but gone, the victims of professional hide hunters.

Roosevelt was just two years out of college , recently married, and launched on a political career as the youngest member of the New York State Assembly. He looked forward to a future as bright as the prospects for western wildlife were grim. Roosevelt realized that the buffalo might soon be extinct, and while a few still remained he ached to experience the thrill of hunting them on horseback, at full gallop, in the sporting tradition so different from the stationary hunting of the commercial hide hunters. When a wealthy New York friend invited him to hunt buffalo on his ranch on the Little Missouri River, in the Bad Lands of North Dakota, he jumped at the chance.

The hunt lasted two weeks. His guide was a local man named Joe Ferris, an ex-lumberjack with the compact strength of a pile driver and a thorough knowledge of the territory. While Roosevelt took to Ferris instantly, the latter had reservations about the dude with his spectacles and high-pitched voice and fancy fringed buckskins. But he was soon won over. Intoxicated by the clear dry air and the rugged landscape of cliffs and buttes, Roosevelt reveled in the hardships of the trail; blistering sun, torrential rains, bogs, quicksand — they were all part of a great adventure. One night, after a drenching shower, as Ferris lay shivering in his wet bedroll, he was astonished to hear his equally soaked client exclaim, *"By Godfrey, this is fun!"*

The dude didn't even mind that they saw very little game. The second day out, Teddy missed a mule deer, but Joe downed it with a follow-up shot. On the sixth day they finally crossed paths with a buffalo, a lone bull that managed to evade them in the maze of coulees and ravines. Later that same afternoon they came upon a trio of bulls. Roosevelt got off a lucky shot at 325 yards that hit one of them in the rump, but it was only a flesh wound. The three animals high-tailed it into the setting sun with Roosevelt and Ferris in mad pursuit. It was almost dark when they finally overtook them. Roosevelt rode up to within twenty feet of the wounded bull and fired again, but poor light and a pitching horse caused him to miss. The bull charged. Teddy's horse wheeled out of the way — a move that slammed T.R.'s rifle against his forehead, opening a deep gash. Blinded by the gushing blood, he heard Ferris get off several shots, but they too went wide.

To their "unutterable chagrin," Roosevelt later recalled, "the wounded bull labored off and vanished into the darkness. I made after him on foot, in hopeless and helpless wrath, until he got out of sight."

Undaunted, they continued on their quest. Several days later, T.R. missed an easy shot at a cow buffalo — it was raining, and his glasses were blurred. Still, it was "one of those misses which a man to his dying day always looks back upon with wonder and regret." That same day, his horse tripped and sent him flying into a thorn bush. Ferris could only shake his head. Bad luck, he declared, seemed to be following them "like a yellow dog follows a drunkard."

Several days later he at last got his buffalo. They had crossed the border into Montana when their horses began nervously to sniff the air. Assuming the nearby presence of a bear or buffalo, Roosevelt dismounted and hiked upwind a hundred yards. He spotted the footprints of a big bull and, glancing over a ridge, saw the animal itself, not fifty yards off. He admired its glossy fall coat and noble bearing, but only for an instant. The bull sensed the hunter's presence and raised its tail, a signal it was about to flee. In a single swift motion, T.R. raised and cocked his Winchester and fired a fatal shot that hit behind the shoulder. He pumped two more shots into the chest as the bull bounded up and over a ridge, blood streaming from its mouth and nostrils. They found it lying dead in the next gully. Ferris looked on in bemused wonder while Roosevelt danced for joy around the carcass.

In his euphoria over shooting the old bull, Roosevelt didn't know — and at the time probably wouldn't have cared — that fewer than a thousand buffalo may have remained in the world. The man who would become our first "environmental president" (to borrow a term coined by George H.W. Bush a century later) was a product of his era, and as yet few voices were being raised in behalf of conservation. When Roosevelt returned to the Bad Lands a year later, in 1884, he seems to have shot at everything that moved; his diary for an extended hunt into the Big Horn Mountains of Montana logs 120 animals killed in a month on the trail, including doves, grouse, sage hens, rabbits, deer, elk, and three grizzlies. Although Roosevelt generally believed in shooting only what he and others could eat, the kill on this hunt was far greater than what he and his guide could consume or pack out.

He was justly proud of the 1,200-pound boar grizzly he dropped with a single shot between the eyes, but he also had no compunction against killing a sow and her cub; the latter, he remarked with clinical detachment, died instantly, "the ball going clean through from end to end." One of Roosevelt's biographers, Edmund Morris, has noted the cold-bloodedness of this and other diary entries for this hunt — "broke the backs" of two black tail bucks; "knocked the heads off 2 grouse"; cut a jackrabbit "nearly in two"; etc. Such statements suggest more than a hunter's pride in killing clean. A letter Roosevelt wrote to his sister hints at what may have been driving him. "I have had good sport," he reported, "and enough excitement and fatigue to prevent overmuch thought."

What he was trying to avoid thinking about was the death, the previous winter, of his twenty-year-old wife in childbirth. Compounding this tragedy, his mother had died on the same day and in the same house. Roosevelt dealt with his grief by throwing himself into a frenzy of activity. The pace of his political life, frenetic to begin with, went into overdrive. It was a presidential election year, and he spent much of it stumping for Republican candidates. Between his campaign commitments he also managed to squeeze three trips to the Bad Lands. He had purchased property there and had begun building a ranch house and stocking the range with cattle. To help run his spread, he imported two hunting guides he had known in Maine. One of these Down-Easters, a huge, burly man named Bill Sewall, complained that he knew more about riding logs than horses and declared the muddy Little Missouri the "meanest apology for a frog pond I ever saw."

Sewall and the other hands on what Roosevelt called his Elkhorn Ranch were amazed by their boss's manic energy. When not overseeing every detail of the operation, he ranged all over the territory, spending whole days in the saddle under a "cloudless glaring sky," as he wrote to his sister, and absorbing the "desolate grim beauty" of the jagged landscape. During rare moments of repose, he would sit in front of his cabin in the evening, watching the hard, gray outlines of the buttes grow soft and purple in the sunset; days, he added, "I spend generally alone, riding through the lonely rolling prairie and broken lands."

Returning east in December, he set to work immediately writing a book on western sport, dashing off nearly 250 pages in a mere nine weeks. Published in 1885, *Hunting Trips of a Ranchman* would be recognized as a definitive text on big-game hunting in the West. It was not, however, without flaws. An anonymous reviewer in *Forest and Stream*, the leading sporting journal of the day, praised the book's vigorous style and the accuracy of its accounts when based on firsthand knowledge, but observed that the author's "limited experience" occasionally caused him to report some "hunting myths" as fact.

Although the review was favorable overall, its mildly critical passages rankled Roosevelt, who called at the New York offices of *Forest and Stream* for an explanation. The offended author calmed down when he learned the review had been written by the magazine's respected editor, George Bird Grinnell, a veteran explorer, naturalist, and hunter who knew the West like few other men.

Nine years older than Roosevelt, Grinnell came from a similar social background. He held a Ph.D. in geology from Yale and was a veteran of scientific expeditions to Yellowstone National Park and other regions of the West. Even more impressive, he had lived with the Pawnees and Blackfeet, had hunted buffalo on horseback with them, and spoke their languages fluently. As a government naturalist, he had ridden with George A. Custer in 1874 on his reconnaissance of the Black Hills. Two years later, Custer invited him to accompany the Seventh Cavalry on its punitive expedition against the Sioux. Pressed by his graduate studies, Grinnell declined, thereby avoiding Custer's fate at the Little Big Horn.

Over the next few years, Roosevelt visited often with Grinnell, engaging him in passionate discussion of the country they loved so much and absorbing the conservation ethic promoted in the pages of *Forest and Stream*. Since its founding in 1876, the magazine had crusaded against the wanton destruction of wildlife, whether by "skin-hunters" or "pseudo-sportsmen," as Grinnell called them, and had pushed for the adoption of conservation laws that would ensure healthy populations of game animals for future generations. Without such laws, Grinnell believed, the demise of the buffalo would be merely the first step in the decimation of all western big-game species; next to go would be elk, deer, antelope, and mountain sheep.

Grinnell's preaching sharpened Roosevelt's awareness of the plight of western game. Until now, he had noted the decline of certain species but had accepted this as a necessary, if regretful, byproduct of westward expansion. By the fall of 1887, however, the situation seemed to have reached a crisis, prompting Roosevelt to action. On a hunt through the Bad Lands that November, he found the range virtually barren of wildlife. Part of this scarcity was due to the devastating cold and blizzards of the previous winter, but he realized that much of it also resulted from overhunting and overgrazing.

Returning to New York in early December, Roosevelt gathered a dozen friends and fellow sportsmen, including Grinnell, for dinner. His purpose: to propose the establishment of a national conservation group, consisting mainly of hunters and named after two of his boyhood heroes, the legendary frontiersmen Daniel Boone and Davy Crockett. The Boone and Crockett Club, its bylaws stated, would work "for the preservation of the large game of this country, further legislation for that purpose, and assist in enforcing existing laws." It would also encourage wilderness exploration, wildlife science, and the preservation of game habitat.

Duly formed and with Roosevelt elected its first president, the club moved swiftly to carry out its mission. During the six years Roosevelt served as president, the club's lobbying efforts led to regulations making Yellowstone National Park a game refuge and protecting it from development. Other accomplishments included the creation of the National Forest system and wildlife reserves in Alaska and California.

It would be as the country's president, of course, that Roosevelt would have his greatest impact on conservation. During his seven and a half years (1901-09) in the White House, he did more for wildlife than any U.S. chief of state before or since. Under his leadership, the government established a national system of wildlife refuges, added five new national parks to the existing one (Yellowstone), implemented the first game laws for Alaska, and increased national forest land five-fold, to 194 million acres.

If Roosevelt's western hunting helped mold him as a conservationist, it was the sum total of his western experience that shaped him as a man of destiny. The West toughened the young Roosevelt, who throughout his early life suffered chronic asthma and indigestion. The extended hunting trips and grueling, month-long roundups (in which T.R. worked as hard as any of his cowhands) added thirty pounds of muscle to his five-foot-eight frame; he later extolled the "fine, healthy life" of a frontier rancher, which "taught a man self-reliance, hardihood, and the vale of instant decision."

The west also democratized this high-born and somewhat snobbish easterner; in North Dakota, Edmund Morris has written, the future president "learned to live on equal terms with men poorer and rougher than himself." The respect he felt toward men like Joe Ferris was mutual. The Dakotans joked about "Old Hasten Forward Quickly There," but they admired this "four-eyed maverick," too, for his energy and leadership; a decade later, at the outbreak of the Spanish-American War, many of them would volunteer for his famous Rough Riders, and some of them would die following him up San Juan Hill.

If it had not been for the years in North Dakota, Roosevelt once remarked, "I never would have become President of the United States."

13

Planting Fish & Playing God

LIVINGSTON STONE WAS NOTHING IF NOT INTREPID. IN JUNE 1873 the Deputy U.S. Fish Commissioner set out from Charlestown, New Hampshire, on a cross-country railroad trip. He was bound for San Francisco with an aquarium car loaded with eight tons of water and ice and a live cargo that included bass, catfish, eels, yellow perch, and brook trout — all fish native to the eastern United States which Stone hoped to establish in the West. But a few miles beyond Omaha the train broke through a trestle and plunged into the Elkhorn River. Stone swam free of the car and climbed to safety atop the engine as it settled into the mud.

Undaunted, the next day he boarded an eastbound train and within three weeks was again heading west, this time with a load of 40,000 Hudson River shad fry in eight ten-gallon cans. The outside temperature varied from below freezing to a hundred degrees, and keeping the water fresh and its temperature within the tolerance range of the fry took constant attention. Stone and his two assistants cooled the water with ice or warmed it with irons heated in the train's fire box. As they crossed the Rockies and Great Basin and climbed the Sierra Nevada they changed the tanks every hour in a vigil that Stone likened to "walking a thousand miles in a thousand hours." Seven days after their departure they deposited the fry — "as fresh and lively as when they left the Hudson River a week before" — into the Sacramento River.

In the 1870s, from a hatchery on California's McCloud River, Livingston Stone shipped the eggs of rainbow trout and king salmon to New York and New Jersey for planting in eastern waters.

This wasn't the first time that American shad, a species of the Atlantic coast, had been planted in Pacific waters. That honor belongs to fish culturist Seth Green, who two years earlier had stocked the Sacramento with 15,000 shad fry. Within a decade of the stockings by Green and Stone, adult shad were returning to the Sacramento to spawn, and by the turn of the century they had spread to rivers from San Diego to Alaska. Today, North America's largest shad run occurs on the Columbia River.

Shad were just the beginning of an exchange that within two decades would transform American fisheries. In the years following the Civil War, advances in the breeding of fish in hatcheries and the completion, in 1869, of the transcontinental railroad set the stage for what amounted to a vast ecological experiment. It was directed by a zealous corps of fish culturists whose spectacular achievements included the transplanting of shad and striped bass to the West Coast, rainbow trout to the East and Midwest, and the introduction of brown trout from Europe.

Mostly these efforts stemmed from the human compulsion

to "improve" on nature, but they were also a response to the devastation of native fisheries wrought by the era's pell-mell industrialization. Sport fishermen rallied to the cause of replacing with new species the brook trout, Michigan grayling, and Atlantic salmon lost to pollution and dams, and they were active in the establishment of state fish commissions to pay for the stockings.

The artificial breeding of fish (presumably carp) began in China several thousand years ago. Its European origins date to the 1300s, when a French monk discovered how to manually fertilize fish eggs and hatch them in sand. Germans and Norwegians were raising trout in hatcheries by the 1780s. In the 1830s, fish culture spread to Britain and from there to the U.S., where in 1853 a Cleveland physician named Theodatus Garlick hatched eggs from brook trout caught near the outlet of Lake Superior. Scores of commercial hatcheries were built in the years immediately following the Civil War. Among their customers were newly created state fish commissions overseeing stocking programs.

In 1870, a group of hatchery owners founded the American Fish Culturists Association. The new organization's purposes included lobbying for the creation of a federal counterpart to the state fish commissions. Congress responded by establishing the U.S. Fish Commission in 1871 and appointed as its head Spencer Fullerton Baird, the respected director of the Smithsonian Institution. The fish-culture movement — "the very first environmental crusade to capture a significant percentage of the American public," according to environmental historian John F. Reiger — was underway.

Three of America's pioneering fish culturists — Stone, Green, and Fred Mather — stand out, not only for their efforts at transplanting fish but for advancing their fledgling science.

Livingston Stone (1836-1912) — Mayflower descendant, Harvard graduate, Unitarian minister, and with Fred Mather one of the five cofounders of the American Fish Culturists Association — started a private hatchery in Charlestown, New Hamp-

In 1871 the fish culturist Seth Green successfully transplanted American shad, an anadromous fish native to the East Coast, to California.

shire. In 1872, as a deputy U.S. Fish Commissioner, he founded the Baird Fish Hatchery on the McCloud River in northern California. Stone oversaw operations there — including the exporting of millions of eggs of rainbow trout and chinook (king) salmon — until 1897.

Seth Green (1817-1888) operated a private hatchery on Caledonia Creek in New York State. An inveterate experimenter in breeding fish, and something of a braggart, Green claimed to have crossed shad and striped bass — a possibility as remote, noted his rival Fred Mather, as mating a horse with a cow. Green did succeed in crossing two closely related char, the spotted or brook trout and the lake trout, thus producing the first "splake," a hardy hybrid still bred and stocked by some state fisheries departments.

Fred Mather (1833-1900) was born in Albany, New York, hunted and trapped in Michigan as a young man, and fought in the Civil War, earning a battlefield commission for gallantry in the Battle of the Wilderness. In 1868 he went into the trout-breeding business at Honeoye Falls, New York. Later, working for the U.S. Fish Commission, he facilitated the exchange of species between America and Europe, and as founder and superintendent of the New York State hatchery at Cold Spring Harbor, Long Island, he bred and distributed the first brown-trout eggs imported from Germany.

Success in the propagation and raising of fish depended on knowledge usually gained on the job. Some species' eggs clumped into balls and resisted mixing with milt. This problem was especially vexing with the eggs of walleyes and bass until methods were developed for removing their sticky coating. Once hatched, fry had to be fed. At his trout hatchery at Honoeye Falls, Mather experimented with chopped boiled eggs and beef, milk curd, and the byproduct of slaughter houses — clotted blood and shredded brains, lungs, and spleens. He finally settled on chopped liver, which he found grew the healthiest trout: "Make it fine at first, coarser as they grow, and crowd it to them," he advised.

Trout and salmon presented fewer problems because their eggs and milt could be easily stripped by hand, and the eggs didn't glom together. Also, the eggs were hardy and could be kept alive for six months if packed in ice, a technique that allowed them to be shipped across continents and oceans without the headaches that went with tending fry on long journeys. British hatcheries were shipping the ova of brown trout and Atlantic salmon to Australia as early as 1864, and in 1868 American brook trout eggs crossed the Atlantic to England.

Two years later, Californians began collecting eggs of the state's native trout from waters near San Francisco and culturing them in several makeshift hatcheries in Berkeley. The first trout eggs to leave the state were sent to Seth Green at Caledonia, New York, in 1875. By then, Livingston Stone had established his hatchery on the McCloud River. Eggs from the trout raised there went east in 1878. Fish culturists in the Golden State called their trout by various names — California red-sided

In the 1880s, Fred Mather imported the eggs of brown trout from Germany and Scotland. A Civil War veteran, he is shown here in the uniform of the Grand Army of the Republic.

trout, California brook trout, California mountain trout — but the name that stuck was rainbow trout.

By the 1880s, rainbows were established in streams throughout the East and Midwest. They were soon sharing waters with their equally adaptable foreign relation, the European brown trout. Credit for the introduction and distribution of browns goes to Fred Mather, who in 1880, as the U.S. representative to an international fisheries exhibition in Berlin, struck up a friendship with Baron Lucius von Behr, the president of the German Fisheries Society. Von Behr took Mather fishing in the Black Forest, and the yellow, brightly spotted trout finning over gravel caught the fancy of his American guest. Von Behr shipped Mather 80,000 brown-trout eggs in 1883 and the next year followed up with another 70,000. Mather forwarded some of the eggs to Seth Green at Caledonia and to a hatchery in Northville, Michigan, and kept others for the state hatchery at Cold Spring Harbor. One of the offspring of the 1883 batch was a big cockfish he named "Herr von Behr," in honor of the Reich's *fischmeister*.

In 1885 more brown-trout eggs made the trans-Atlantic trip, this time from Loch Levin, Scotland. The Teutonic and Scottish varieties had different markings. German browns sported a yellow-gold body adorned with black and red bulls-eye spots, while Loch Levin browns bore a more salmonlike appearance, with a silver body and smaller, black spots. For a time, fish culturists tried to keep the two varieties segregated and to stock them in separate waters, and even today some anglers boast of the brightly marked "German" browns in their local streams.

In a similar vein, others may talk about particular rivers holding "pure" McCloud rainbows. But we must take with a ration of salt most such claims about trout pedigrees. Von Behr's trout represented two different strains of browns, one from lakes and the other from streams, and from the beginning they were crossbred in U.S. hatcheries. Undoubtedly, crossbreeding between the German and Loch Levin browns, and later between their descendants and brown trout from England, also occurred. The McCloud fish had mixed parentage, too. Stone crossed resident rainbows with McCloud River steelhead, their sea-run cousins, and in the East their offspring almost certainly bred with the Berkeley strain that had arrived in 1875. In turn, descendants of these fish were later bred with rainbow stocks from other rivers in California and Oregon. As befitting America's melting-pot heritage, our browns and rainbows are richly polyglot.

Last but not least among the fish culturists' contributions was the transplanting of striped bass to California. This East Coast native breeds in fresh or brackish water and prowls the surf and estuaries between the Carolinas and Nova Scotia. After Stephen Roush Throckmorton, the chief of the California Fish Commission, hooked into a few linesiders on a trip east, he talked to Livingston Stone about acquiring some brood stock. On orders from Stone, in June 1879 a U.S. Fish Commission employee named Harry Mason netted 167 juvenile stripers in New Jersey's Navesink River and sent them cross-country by train. The 107 that survived were deposited into San Francisco Bay. Another 300 Navesink stripers joined them in 1882. By the turn of the century, stripers roamed the western littoral from San Diego to Vancouver, and their annual commercial harvest topped a million pounds.

Not every action by the U.S. Fish Commission proved an unalloyed blessing, however. Its most dubious "success" was the European carp, whose introduction seemed like a great idea at the time. Carp had been imported earlier in the century but confined to a few private ponds, and their widespread distribution did not occur until 1876, when von Behr convinced Spencer Baird they were just what America needed.

In Germany carp had long been a popular food fish, sold live from tubs by street vendors. In many ways they are indeed a wonder fish. Although mainly vegetarian, carp will eat most anything. They can survive water temperatures ranging from near freezing to ninety-six degrees, grow ten pounds in three years, and are wildly prolific. Von Behr shipped Baird 345 adult carp. The stock soon outgrew the Baltimore ponds where he had them placed, and when some were moved to ponds in the District of Columbia, politicians took notice. The fish commissioner made extravagant claims for the fat bottom-grubbers, pushing them as a ready source of protein which farmers could raise more cheaply than pigs.

A kind of carp mania ensued as congressmen sent them by the trainload to constituents in the hustings. But the carp boom soon went bust. Farmers found no market for them, their feeding habits muddied waters, and they crowded out native fish. Officials declared open season on carp and tried to eradicate them by netting and poisoning, to little effect.

Fred Mather, who served for years as Baird's assistant, lamented the bad judgment of his otherwise estimable boss. No fish, he rued, "is so heartily cursed by Americans."

The carp fiasco would be repeated many times with the importing of other exotic animals and plants, from starlings to killer bees to kudzu. Even "good" fish transplants could have negative effects. The first American stream stocked with German browns was Michigan's Pere Marquette, and once established, they contributed to the extinction of its native grayling. In other waters, browns and rainbows shoved aside indigenous brook and cutthroat trout. In many eastern streams, however, logging and industry had already killed off the resident brookies, and the new species coped better with the degraded environment. At least as often, planted fish took hold in ecological niches that nature had yet to fill. Until humans stocked them, for example, many high-country waters in the Rocky Mountains were barren of trout, and the dam-building frenzy that gripped the U.S. in the mid-twentieth century created virgin lakes for largemouth bass, walleye, and freshwater strains of striped bass (a record striper from California's San Luis Reservoir weighed 67 pounds, 8 ounces). Another conspicuously successful case of fisheries managers enhancing nature was the planting, beginning in the 1890s, of Pacific salmon and steelhead in the Great Lakes.

The stocking of non-native species continued apace for more than a century, transforming fisheries throughout the world. Today, wild populations of rainbow and brown trout — originally confined to western North America and Europe, respectively — can be found throughout the United States and on every continent except Antarctica and Greenland. In my own peregrinations I have caught gem-spotted browns above tree line on Mount Kenya and rainbows under the gaze of Incan ruins in Peru. Far from their ancestral waters of Labrador, some of the largest brook trout on earth cruise lakes in Argentina. Ferocious peacock bass, native to South America, now prowl Florida waters. A globetrotting angler can pursue largemouth bass, a native of the southern U.S., in Africa, Central America, and Australia.

From the days of Fred Mather and Seth Green the try-anything approach usually prevailed, with little thought given to the possibility that stocking exotic species could depress populations of native fish or even drive them to extinction. This is a concern in Yellowstone Lake, where lake trout illegally introduced by anglers threaten indigenous cutthroat trout. Yesterday's attempts to improve on nature is today's ecological vandalism.

Unhampered by environmental impact statements, the hatchery men pursued their mission with bracing innocence. In time, of course, there emerged a new ethic that challenged this unquestioning manipulation of nature. Livingston Stone, for one, came to see the limitations of stocking and argued for conservation, including the establishment of a salmon sanctuary in Alaska.

When we ponder the pluses and minuses of indiscriminate stocking and how attitudes have changed over the years, it's instructive to look at the Delaware River — one of many examples one could cite. Three centuries ago it held just three species we would regard as sport fish — brook trout, shad, and striped bass. Today an angler on the Delaware can still catch those three, as well as smallmouth and largemouth bass, rock bass, bluegills, walleyes, muskellunge, and brown and rainbow trout. Brook trout are rare and relegated to the Delaware's headwaters, but the other species flourish, largely because of conservation efforts begun in the 1960s to clean up the river after years of abuse.

In the 1870s a New Jersey fish culturist named John H. Slack (1834-1874) introduced salmon to the Delaware and actually established a short-lived run. Along with Livingston Stone and Fred Mather, Slack was a cofounder of the American Fish Culturists Association. Like Stone he was a deputy U.S. Fish Commissioner who worked tirelessly in behalf of Spencer Baird's vision. At his Troutdale hatchery, near Bloomsbury, New Jersey, Slack raised chinook salmon hatched from eggs shipped overland from Stone's hatchery in California as well as Atlantic salmon from eggs sent to him from Maine, Canada, and Germany. The salmon fry raised at Troutdale went into the Delaware and other eastern rivers, including the Raritan, Susquehanna, and Potomac, although returns were recorded only for the Delaware.

Slack and later his wife, Thirza, who continued the stockings after his untimely death, at age thirty-nine, released more than 2 million fry into the Delaware between 1873 and 1878. Returning salmon were first observed in 1875. The numbers steadily increased through 1878; in April of that year, commercial shad fishermen working upstream of Trenton landed a 42-inch, 23-pound Atlantic salmon in their nets. The great fish was sent on ice to Washington, where a triumphant Spencer Baird showed it off to President Rutherford B. Hayes and influential members of Congress.

It was the high-water mark of Baird's grand experiment: the Delaware had another good run in 1879, but in the words of a report by the state fisheries commission, "the experiences of that year were not repeated." In 1880 just a few adults were recorded, and in 1881 a few were reported but none confirmed. As probable cause of the experiment's failure, the commission observed "that in the late summer and early autumn, the waters of the Delaware are usually very low, and of a higher temperature than that of rivers to which the salmon is indigenous."

In the 1980s, the N.J. Division of Fish and Game cited the partial success of Slack's efforts when it proposed stocking the Delaware with chinook salmon. Sport fishermen, who even a decade earlier might have embraced the idea, arose in near-unanimous opposition, and in 1992 the project was shelved. The Delaware already had a great sport fishery, they argued. Why mess with it?

14

Call Me Nessmuk

"To myself I sometimes appear as a wild Indian or an old Berserker, masquerading under the guise of a nineteenth century American. When the strait jacket of civilization becomes too oppressive, I throw it off, betake myself to savagery, and there loaf and refresh my soul. . . . I love a horse, a gun, a dog, a trout and a pretty girl. I hate a pothunter, a trout-liar and a whiskey-guzzling sportsman. I smoke and take an occasional glass of wine and never lie about my hunting and fishing exploits more than the occasion seems to demand."

So George Washington Sears described himself. Writing under the pen name Nessmuk, Sears through most of the 1880s was the star correspondent for *Forest and Stream*, the nation's premier outdoor publication. His articles on canoeing, camping, hunting, and fishing brought pleasure to thousands of sportsmen while educating them, at a time when conservation was still in its infancy, about the destruction of the nation's woodlands and fisheries.

Sears capped his reputation in dispatches he filed during three paddle-and-portage trips through New York's Adirondack wilderness. He made these journeys in successively smaller canoes built for him by J. Henry Rushton of Canton, New York. The last, dubbed the *Sairy Gamp* after a tippler in a Dickens novel who "took no water," was just nine feet long and weighed 10½ pounds. On the eve of Sears's departure, Rushton joked

George Washington Sears, alias Nessmuk, entertained his "Grand Army of 'Outers'" in dispatches from his canoeing trips in the Adirondack Mountains of New York State. We go into the woods not to rough it, he wrote, but "to smooth it."

that if he got tired of the *Sairy Gamp* as a canoe he could "use it for a soup dish."

Although scarcely bigger than a toy, the *Sairy Gamp* proved practical enough for the diminutive Sears, who stood five-foot-three and weighed 105 pounds. Buck naked, said his friend Fred Mather, he looked like a bar of soap "after a hard day's washing." The tiny craft also fit Sears's minimalist philosophy about camping. He carried just fifteen pounds of gear and food — a light tent, an extra shirt and socks, a blanket bag, knapsack, knife, hatchet, compass, rifle, fishing rod, a tin kettle and dish, and some coffee and beans. "Go light," he told his readers, "the lighter the better."

In his own words, Sears had "a liking for adventure, intense love of nature in her wildest dress, and a strange fondness for being in deep forests by myself." From early age he exhibited an independent spirit, one that "could *not bear* restraint or confinement." The son of a cobbler (a trade he would grudgingly take up) and the oldest of ten children, he was born in Webster, Massachusetts, in 1821. When his father sent him to work in a cotton mill at age eight, he ran away to live with a local band of Nipmuc Indians. Among them was a man who taught him all he knew about woodcraft. Sears soaked up this wilderness knowledge and later, when he began writing about the outdoors, he took as a byline his mentor's name — Nessmuk — which in Algonquin means wood drake. As Sears ruefully noted, he inherited from his namesake "all his love for forest life, and alas, much of his good-natured shiftlessness."

Sears returned to the hated mill, but by twelve he was apprenticed to his father while working summers as a commercial fisherman on Cape Cod. At nineteen he went to sea on a whaling ship. After three years in the South Pacific "cruisin' for sperm," as he put it, he settled down, after his fashion, as a shoemaker in Brockport, New York, and then Wellsboro, Pennsylvania, where he moved in 1848. But the wilderness always beckoned, and even after marrying, at age thirty-six, and starting a family he would abandon his cobbler's bench for months at a stretch for life in the woods, often far from home. He trapped in Ontario and Minnesota and spent several seasons as a professional hunter in Michigan, supplying railroad construction crews with venison. Many details of his life are hazy, but he claimed to have a been a teamster on the plains, a teacher in Ohio, a silver miner in Colorado, a cowboy in Texas, and "a webfoot in Oregon."

During the Civil War he served briefly in a Pennsylvania sharpshooter regiment, and he later made two trips to Brazil. Ostensibly he went there to investigate the rubber trade, but one gleans that his real purpose was to scratch another itch. Guided by the Brazilian journal of the Swiss naturalist Louis Agassiz, he explored the Amazon and several of its tributaries.

Although his formal education stopped with grade school, Sears was a voracious reader all his life — he boasted of carrying in his head "a sufficient supply of Shakespeare, Pope, Byron and Burns." He also devoured Dickens. And like every American writer of his generation, he was influenced by philosopher Ralph Waldo Emerson's call to follow your inner voice. A reader can hear in his writings echoes of Walt Whitman's *Leaves of Grass* and Herman Melville's *Moby Dick.* (Sears and Melville shipped on whalers the same year, 1841, out of New Bedford, Massachusetts.) We don't know if he read the works of Henry David Thoreau, but his life epitomized a famous line in *Walden*, "If a man does not keep pace with his companions, it is perhaps because he hears a different drummer."

SEARS'S CAREER AS A WRITER began in 1860, when he published, for the first time under the pen name Nessmuk, a series of articles in *Porter's Spirit of the Times*, an outdoor magazine that ceased publishing a year later, a victim of the Civil War. (The founder was Frank Forester's friend William T. Porter.) Over the next ten years he wrote poetry for *The Atlantic Monthly* and other publications, and he briefly edited Wellsboro's newspaper. Sears found writing enjoyable, he said, but "not remunerative," and with a wife and three children to support he rededicated himself to shoemaking and put down the pen, he thought for good.

He might have lived out the rest of his life in obscurity were it not for a letter published in 1879 in *Forest and Stream* in which a reader asked, Whatever happened to Nessmuk? The query spurred Sears to write the editor, Charles Hallock, informing him he was still alive and eager to take up writing again. Over the next decade he would publish ninety-four articles in *Forest and Stream*, eighteen as "letters" describing his three trips through the Adirondacks in Henry Rushton's canoes.

Rushton's first canoe for Sears, named the *Wood Drake* and built for his 1880 voyage, was ten feet long and weighed less than eighteen pounds. He followed this with a sixteen-pound boat, the *Susan Nipper* (like the *Sairy Gamp*, named for a character in Dickens), which Sears took into the wilderness in 1881. The sixty-year-old Sears sat out the 1882 season because of ill health — he had long suffered from asthma and was probably in the early stages of tuberculosis, a disease that eventually killed him — but in 1883 he felt well enough to launch a six-week, 266-mile voyage in the *Sairy Gamp.*

This third canoe for Sears was the finest Rushton had ever built. Although just eighteen inches shorter that the *Susan Nipper* and two inches less in beam, at ten pounds, eight ounces it was 25 percent lighter — Sears could easily lift it with one hand, yet it floated him and all his gear with a comfortable five inches of freeboard.

The key to the *Sairy Gamp*'s strength were thirty-nine closely arrayed ribs of split red-elm dowels; to this framework Rushton used copper rivets to attach, lengthwise, twelve strips of cedar lapstake. Its maker proclaimed the *Sairy Gamp* "the smallest, lightest craft that ever floated a man," albeit a small one. Rushton worried that under the stress of wilderness travel his untested creation might "go to pieces like an eggshell," but when Sears returned it the following fall he had nothing but praise for its performance: "I have smashed her, rocked her, got her onto spruce knots, and been rattled down rapids stern foremost; and I have sent her back, as tight and staunch as the day I took her. . . . I was trying to find out how light a canoe it took to drown a man. I never shall know."

THE 1883 CRUISE MARKED the height of Sears's popularity. Throughout that summer, readers of the weekly *Forest and Stream* followed Nessmuk in the reports he posted from tourist hotels and villages along his route, and the mainstream press also picked up his story.

Forest and Stream made the most of its celebrated writer by publishing, in 1884, a book that encapsulated his fifty-plus years as an outdoorsman. *Woodcraft and Camping*, which remains in print to this day, is one of the classics of outdoor writing. Sears's prose, like Thoreau's, is flinty and direct and reads as well now as it did more than a century ago. Sometimes writing in the third person as the Old Woodsman, or O.W., he poked gentle fun at the younger city sports he occasionally guided. He instructed readers on how to build a fire, erect a shanty-tent, cook a Johnnycake, stuff a camp pillow, and catch a frog.

To keep mosquitoes and black flies at bay he prescribed a recipe for "punkie dope" whose primary ingredients were pine and castor oil. "Rub it in thoroughly and liberally at first," he instructed, "and after you have established a good glaze, a little replenishing from day to day will be sufficient. . . . A good safe coat of this varnish grows better the longer it is kept on. . . . Last summer I carried a cake of soap and a towel in my napsack through the North Woods for a seven weeks' tour, and never used either a single time." A good thing, perhaps, that the O.W. preferred camping alone.

More wisdom from *Woodcraft and Camping*:

Camps: Keep them simple, Sears advised. He liked a plain "Indian camp" — basically a lean-to made on the spot by cutting a hemlock sapling, leaning it against a bigger tree, and draping it with branches cut from another hemlock. A more elaborate shelter could be built of canvas, so long as it was open on one side and faced "the cheerful, healthful light and warmth of a camp-fire." Avoid enclosed tents, "in which one is required to seclude himself through the hours of sleep in damp and darkness."

Campfires: "The way in which an average party of summer outers will contrive to manage — or mis-manage — the camp and camp-fire so as to get the greatest amount of smoke and discontent at the least outlay of time and force, is something past all understanding."

Camp cooking: "It is probably true that nothing connected with outdoor life in camp is so badly botched as the cooking." The plainest cooking "is the best, so that it be well done and wholesome." He detested flapjacks and dismissed as "effeminate luxuries" canned salmon, tomatoes, and peaches.

Hunting: "Hunters, like poets, are born, not made. The art cannot be taught on paper." Rather than stalking, Sears preferred "the art of sitting on a log." When hunting this way, "swear yourself black in the face never to shoot at a dim, moving object in the woods for a deer, unless you have seen that it is a deer. In these days there are quite as many hunters as deer in the woods; and it is a heavy, wearisome job to pack a dead or wounded man ten or twelve miles out to a clearing, let alone that it spoils all the pleasure of the hunt, and is apt to raise hard feelings among his relations."

FISHING: Sears claimed to prefer fly fishing, but he was no snob about it, and he would angle with "worms, grubs, minnows, grasshoppers, crickets, and any sort of doodle bug." He enjoyed himself "hugely catching catties on a dark night from a skiff with a hand-line." He also advocated bending down the barbs of hooks for better penetration (not for catch-and-release, a then unknown concept).

FROGGING: Sears confessed to a "weakness" for snaring bullfrogs by any means necessary, whether spearing, snagging, or jacklighting from a canoe at night. He advised using "a good headlight" and to "paddle up to him silently and throw the light on his eyes; you may then pick him up as you would a potato." In daylight he preferred catching them on a hook and line with a bit of scarlet flannel as bait. Paddle up "behind and silently, and drop the rag just in front of his nose. He is pretty certain to take it on the instant. Knock him on the head before cutting off his legs." Otherwise, it "is unpleasant to see him squirm, and hear him cry like a child while you saw at his thigh joints." For Sears, frog legs as camp fare commanded "first place for delicacy and flavor," an opinion not universally shared. When one "old pork-gobbling back woodsman" learned that Sears had cooked frog legs in a particular frying pan, he threw it in the river.

Much of the advice in *Woodcraft and Camping* is dated — in our era of low-impact camping, a backpacker will blanche at Sears's suggestions to cut hemlock browse for bedding and to fell whole trees for fires and shelters, and a hunter could risk arrest by following his recommendations for jacklighting. But the author's vision and spirit endure. Sears lamented the scarcity of effective game laws and the environmental destruction wrought by the nation's rapid industrialization; although his livelihood depended on making shoes, he railed at the construction of a tannery near his home which "poisons and blackens the stream with chemicals, bark and ooze." He dedicated *Woodcraft and Camping* to "the Grand Army of 'Outers'" seeking refuge from the "hurry and worry" of urban life, and he taught them to be at home in the outdoors. "We do not go to the green woods and crystal waters to rough it," he pronounced, "we go to smooth it."

Age and illness slowed his output, but Sears continued writing for *Forest and Stream*. He reported on two long excursions to the wild east coast of central Florida; for one of these Rushton built him a canoe that was six inches shorter and nine ounces lighter than the *Sairy Gamp*. Following his practice, Sears camped alone on the Halifax River, where he loafed, fished, and hunted wild turkey and quail. Of the latter, he wrote, "I always felt a little ashamed of murdering such cute, beautiful things for a few ounces of meat; knowing in my conscience that hog and hominy were quite as good fare as I deserved."

He returned to Wellsboro in April 1887 from what proved to be his last journey afield. Sears was sixty-five but felt much older, and in addition to his asthma and tuberculosis he now suffered from malaria. Enfeebled by age and illness, by the spring of 1890 he was too weak to leave his house without assistance. His family set up a tent in the yard so he could at least camp with his grandchildren. He died on the first of May. A nonconformist to the last, Sears had asked for the sake of science to be autopsied, and in lieu of a funeral he requested that his bones be articulated and preserved "where the blessed sunlight can sometimes reach them." Ignoring these wishes, his survivors gave him a proper burial in a grove of hemlocks near his house. Two years later his remains were removed to the local cemetery, and in 1893 a monument funded by readers of *Forest and Stream* was erected over his grave. Visitors can see it still, and in the Wellsboro area the memory of "Nessmuk" also lives on in the name of a lake and a mountain.

"Tempus fugit," the ailing Sears wrote to a friend a few years before his death. "Let him fly; let him flicker. I have been there, and done it."

15

Ishi: America's Last Wild Indian

By the spring of 1914 strollers in San Francisco's golden Gate Park had become familiar with a curious scene. Two men — one slim and distinguished looking in a suit and tie, the other dark and stocky, in khaki work clothes and with hair pulled back in a ponytail — were practicing archery. The man in the suit watched the other carefully as he crouched, notched an arrow, and sent it flying low over the grass. His motion was swift and sure, and as the arrow thudded into the ground some fifty yards away he drew another from his otter-skin quiver and fired again. Other bows lay on the ground, and soon both men were shooting them from the same crouched position while talking excitedly in pidgin English.

The park visitors who paused to watch this odd pair were witnessing the birth of modern bowhunting. The man in the suit was Dr. Saxton Pope, a professor of surgery at the Berkeley Medical School. His companion and teacher was Ishi, a Yana Indian who had spent most of his life hiding from white men in the remote Northern California wilderness.

Ishi had caused a sensation two and a half years before, when he had walked out of the foothills below Mount Lassen and surrendered himself to the white society he had feared and avoided since childhood. His emaciated frame draped in a scrap of ancient covered-wagon canvas, he was found cowering in the corral of a slaughterhouse and offered no resistance when the sheriff at Oroville locked him up in the county jail. The locals filed through the jail to gaze in wonder at the "wild man" who appeared to speak neither English, Spanish, nor any of the local Indian languages.

Reports in San Francisco newspapers of the wild Indian's capture drew the attention of Berkeley anthropologists Alfred Kroeber and Thomas Waterman, the latter an authority on California native languages. When Waterman hurried to the Oroville jail to examine its strange captive, he brought with him a vocabulary of the Yana, a tribe of hunter-gatherers thought to have been wiped out by settlers in the previous century. To Waterman's astonishment, the Indian responded to a few of the words, his face lighting up in recognition. *Siwini!* he exclaimed, repeating the Yana word for yellow pine while knocking on the pine framework of his cell cot. *Siwini!*

He had reason enough for excitement, for as Waterman learned, it had been three years since the Indian had last communicated with another human being. After Waterman recruited one of two surviving civilized Yanas as an interpreter, the man's story began unfolding. He was about fifty years old and the last of the Yani, the southernmost of the three Yana groups that had occupied Northern California at the time of the 1849 gold rush. With the influx of miners and settlers had come inevitable conflict and the decimation of his people. By 1875 only about sixteen Yani remained alive, concealed in the nearly inaccessible canyons on the lower slopes of Mount Lassen. Over the years, the group's numbers dwindled further until only two, the Indian in the Oroville jail and his aged mother, remained. When she died, in the fall of 1908, he was utterly alone.

Ishi — this was the name given to him by Waterman, after the Yana word for "man" — carried on as best he could for several more years. In growing despair and with nothing to live for, he came out of the hills on August 29, 1911, and placed himself at the mercy of the white invaders whose diseases, bullets, and

Ishi, the last of the Yani Indians, walked out of the California foothills in 1911. Befriended by several Berkeley professors, he learned English, worked as a janitor at the university, and demonstrated wilderness skills like fire-making (right) and hunting with a bow and arrow.

vigilante's noose had all but exterminated his tribe.

By now, attitudes toward Indians had changed in California, and the ragged, lonely figure behind bars evoked curiosity rather than fear and hatred. The *saltu*, or whites, whom he assumed would kill him instead treated him kindly. He had the added good fortune of being adopted by Kroeber and Waterman, anthropologists with a pronounced sympathy for, as well as professional interest in, California Indian cultures. The two Berkeley professors arranged to have Ishi released in their custody and brought him to San Francisco and the Berkeley Museum of Anthropology.

To their great surprise (and no doubt to Ishi's too), their Yani charge made a remarkable adjustment to civilization. He was put on the museum payroll as an assistant janitor, a job he performed with skill and obvious pride. He learned enough English to shop in the local markets and to explore the city on its cable cars. Newspapers wrote features about him. He became a celebrity and a kind of living exhibit at the museum.

Kroeber and Waterman interviewed Ishi at length, taking careful notes of everything he told them about his language, culture, and wilderness life. Many memories of the long hiding were painful, and Ishi recalled them with difficulty. But he was always happy to show them how he made bows and arrows. Sometimes he would wander out into the field behind the museum to work on his hunting weapons. On one of these occasions he was joined by Dr. Saxton Pope, whose life would be changed forever by the experience.

Pope and Ishi already knew each other slightly. The medical school was next door to the museum, and Ishi had been a patient there several times; like all aborigines, he was highly susceptible to white respiratory diseases. A year after Ishi had taken up residence at the museum, Pope was gazing out of his office window when he saw the Indian fashioning a bow. Fascinated, he came outside for a closer look. Pleased at the attention, Ishi was soon showing Pope his shooting stance and method of release. From the museum the two men wandered a few blocks to the grassy edge of the Sutro Forest, an undeveloped park in the center of the city, where Ishi continued his impromptu archery lesson.

So began one of the most remarkable friendships in the history of field sports. "It would be difficult, truly, to say which of the two meant the most to the other," Kroeber's widow, Theodora, wrote years later. "Popey," as Ishi called him, had a strong romantic streak and was taken by the notion of having, literally as his next-door neighbor, this "wild" yet remarkably gentle Indian who had spent all his life in a state of nature. He would grow to love him as a brother. Ishi, for his part, looked on Pope as a powerful *ku wi*, or shaman, less for his surgical skills, apparently, than for his adeptness at sleight-of-hand tricks.

Watching Ishi, Pope became enthralled with the possibilities of bow hunting as a sport. Under Ishi's tutelage, he became a skilled hunter in his own right. His first forays were for small game such as rabbits and quail, but before long he was bagging bigger fare, including deer, cougar, and Kodiak bear. Eventually, with a younger colleague named Arthur Young, he became one of the first white men to hunt and kill African big game with a bow. He introduced the excitement and challenge of bowhunting to thousands of sportsmen through books as well as articles in *Field & Stream* and other outdoor magazines. The name of the Pope and Young Club, the record-keeper for North American big game taken with a bow, honors their pioneering contributions to the sport.

Ishi was a meticulous craftsmen, and as his protégé observed, he "loved his bow as he loved nothing else in his possession." He made the bow, or *man-nee*, from a short, flat piece of mountain juniper, cut with an obsidian knife from a standing tree, recurved over a fire, and scraped smooth with sandstone. Sinew from the leg tendons of a deer served as backing and was attached with glue boiled from salmon skin. Tendons from the deer's shank were chewed until soft and twisted into a cord to make the bowstring.

The arrow, or *sa wa*, was cut from witch-hazel. New shafts about thirty-two inches long were bound together and cured for a month or longer. From these, Ishi would select the truest, cut them back to twenty-six inches, and add a six-inch foreshaft of heavier mountain mahogany. He painted the shafts with pigments made from natural sources — red from cinnabar, black from a trout's eye, green from wild onions, blue from a plant root — all mixed with resin and applied with a stick. The arrow was fledged with the wing feathers of an eagle, hawk, or flicker (avoiding owl feathers as bad medicine). Finally, an arrowhead struck from obsidian was inserted into the foreshaft, glued with pine resin, and lashed tight with sinew.

Pope learned to craft his own bows and went on to explore the technology and history of archery, becoming the world's leading authority on the subject. After experimenting with various models, he declared the English longbow superior to Ishi's weapons, but Ishi demurred: "Too much *man-nee*." Pope also adopted the English shooting style, holding the bow vertically and drawing the arrow back to the ear. Again, Ishi remained unimpressed and stuck with what Pope termed his "Mongolian release." In this method, the bow is held loosely in the palm and on a diagonal with the ground, the arrow resting on the heel of the palm and guided between the thumb and index finger. Ishi usually shot from a crouch and drew the bow back only to the chest.

When they shot together on a target range, Pope was surprised to find Ishi an indifferent marksman. The doctor regularly beat his friend at targets, prompting Ishi to repaint his arrows in different colors for better luck. In the field where it counted, however, he was a deadly shot. Pope gasped at his ability to drop a ground squirrel at forty yards, while from the same distance he could completely miss a conventional bull's-eye target. Ishi explained that the target was distractingly large and that the colored rings diverted his attention.

In the spring of 1914, Ishi returned to his old hunting grounds on Deer and Mill creeks, below Mount Lassen. With Kroeber ("Chiep," or chief, as he called him), Waterman ("Watamany"), Popey, and Pope's eleven-year-old son he passed a month-long idyll in the land of his ancestors, hunting and fishing and living off the land. Kroeber had wanted to make the trip for several years to observe Ishi in his native state. At first Ishi demurred; he had made a happy adjustment to civilization, and the old country was filled with spirits of the dead. But with prodding he reluctantly agreed to go.

Once they were in the mountains and surrounded by the sounds and smells of the chaparral, Ishi's attitude changed. The catharsis of reliving the old days of his long concealment was softened by the presence of his friends and the wonderful time they obviously were having. Ishi reverted to bare feet and breech clout, while Popey and the rest went one step further, stripping entirely to the buff. Ishi disapproved, less out of modesty than for such practical concerns as poison oak and sunburn. He was less than pleased, too, when Popey and Chiep broke a Yahi taboo by killing a rattlesnake, then compounded the sin by cooking and eating it.

In the main, however, what Ishi had initially called this "crazy-aunatee treep" proved happy for all concerned. They swam in the ice-cold creeks and told stories by the evening's campfire, where they also sang and danced, accompanied by Popey's guitar. Ishi and Popey were the official hunters and kept the party supplied with game. Working with his Yahi mentor daily in the field, Pope in the space of a few weeks absorbed a lifetime's wilderness lore. "Hunting with Ishi was pure joy," he recalled. "Bow in hand, he seemed to be transformed into a being light as air and as silent as falling snow."

Ishi was unfailingly scrupulous in his preparation for the hunt. As Pope explained,

> He would eat no fish the day before the hunt, and smoke no tobacco, for these odors are detected a great way off. He rose early, bathed in the creek, rubbed himself with the aromatic leaves of yerba buena, washed out his mouth, drank water, but ate no food. … From the very edge of camp, until he returned, he was on the alert for game, and the one obvious element of his mental attitude was that he suspected game everywhere. He saw a hundred objects that looked like deer, to every live animal in reality. He took it for granted that ten deer see you where you see one — so see it first. On the trail, it was a crime to speak. His warning note was a soft, low whistle or a hiss. As he walked, he placed every footfall with precise care; the most stealthy step I ever saw.

Ishi hunted in breech clout and bare feet — clothes made too much noise, he said, and a naked man was sensitive to every twig he brushed against. Ishi's senses were so acute that Pope swore he could *smell* deer, cougar, and foxes, and often discovered them this way.

He could lure all manner of beasts into arrow range by imitating their calls. Fingers against his lips produced a "plaintive squeak like a rabbit caught by a hawk." Soon, rabbits from up to a hundred yards away would appear, moving cautiously to within ten or fifteen yards "while Ishi dragged out his squeak in a most pathetic manner. Then he would shoot." When Pope tested Ishi's calling in twelve different locations one afternoon, he produced on command five jackrabbits and a wildcat. "He could imitate the call of a quail to such an extent that he spoke a half-dozen sentences to them. He knew the crow of the cock on sentinel duty when he signals to others; he knew the cry of warning, and the run-to-shelter cry of the hen: her command to her little ones to fly; and the 'lie low' cluck; then at last the 'all's well' chirp."

Pope observed how Ishi called deer in the fawn season "by placing a folded leaf between his lips and sucking vigorously. This made a bleat such as a lamb gives, or a boy makes blowing on a blade of grass between his thumbs." He also attracted deer with a stuffed buck's head. Ishi wore the decoy as a cap, "bobbing up and down behind bushes" to excite a deer's curiosity.

"Not only could Ishi call the animals, but he could understand their language," observed Pope. "Often when we have been hunting he has stopped and said, 'The squirrel is scolding a fox.' At first I said to him, 'I don't believe you.' Then he would say, 'Wait! Look!' Hiding behind a tree or rock or bush, in a few minutes we would see a fox trot across the open forest."

Sometimes Ishi would stop on the trail and tell Pope it was no use going farther. A bluejay, he said, had reported their presence, so that all the animals were alerted. Concluded Pope, "Only a white hunter would advance under these circumstances."

In addition to his repertoire of stalking and calling skills, Ishi exhibited extraordinary patience. He never gave up, Pope noted, "when he knew a rabbit was in a clump of brush. Time meant nothing to him; he simply stayed until he got his game. He would watch a squirrel hole for an hour if necessary, but he always got his squirrel."

Exhilarated by their month in the wilds, Popey and the rest of Ishi's friends dreamed of repeating it. They never did. The following December, Ishi came down with a persistent cough, another in the series of respiratory infections that had plagued him from the beginnings of his sojourn among the *saltu.* It was the first stage of tuberculosis. For the next fifteen months he battled the disease valiantly but at last succumbed. Pope attended him daily, and he had the best care possible in the Berkeley hospital.

As his time approached, Ishi insisted on being home at the museum when called to the Spirit World. An exhibit room was cleared for him. Large and sunny, it looked out over Golden Gate Park and the Sutro Forest, where he and Popey had spent so many delightful afternoons with their bows and arrows. Cheerful and uncomplaining to the end, he died on March 15, 1916. His *ku wi* and best friend, Popey, was by his side.

Ishi was cremated according to Yana custom. In the coffin, his friends placed items he would need for the journey ahead: some acorn meal, dried venison, tobacco, shell money, obsidian flakes, a bow, and five arrows.

"He looked upon us as sophisticated children — smart, but not wise," Pope wrote in a testimonial. "We knew many things and much that is false. He knew nature, which was always true. . . . With him there was no word for goodbye. He said: 'You stay, I go.' He was gone and he hunts with his people. We stay, and he has left us with the heritage of the bow."

16

Carl Akeley: Michelangelo of Taxidermy

In an encounter perhaps unique in the annals of hunting, Carl Akeley once killed a leopard with his bare hands. It happened in British Somaliland (today's Somalia), in 1896. Akeley, a thirty-two-year-old taxidermist whose name would one day be immortalized in two great halls of African mammals (one in New York's American Museum of Natural History, the other in Chicago's Field Museum) was on his first expedition to Africa. He was returning to camp after a long, hot day of hunting in the arid bushland when he glimpsed, thirty yards off to his right, a shadowy form moving through thick brush. Instinctively he raised his rifle and fired.

An unmistakable snarl told him what he had hit. He cursed. It was past sunset, and in the gathering dusk he could no longer make out his rifle sights — no time to be tangling with a wounded leopard. When the leopard moved out from behind the brush, Akeley got off three more rounds, to no apparent effect.

The leopard charged, bounding the twenty yards between them in a heart-stopping instant, and with a tremendous leap smashed into Akeley. Man and beast hit the ground, locked in a furious embrace. The leopard sank its teeth into Akeley's arm and with its hind legs ripped at his stomach. Akeley, who had lost his rifle on contact, managed to roll the leopard and get a grip on its neck with one hand while thrusting a fist down its throat. He pressed his knees against the leopard's chest and felt

Carl Akeley posing with the leopard he killed in a hand-to-paw fight in Somaliland in 1896.

one rib crack, then another. Akeley held on as its life slowly ebbed. The leopard trembled and at last lay still.

The tenacity and single-mindedness Akeley showed in his tangle with the leopard were qualities he also brought to his life's work. No one has had a greater influence on taxidermy. His innovative methods for mounting elephants and other large game were revolutionary. Before Akeley, no one had ever mounted specimens with such fidelity. The realism of his "habitat groups" — dioramas showing game animals in their natural settings, with backgrounds painted on curved walls to suggest depth — made viewers gasp. Akeley's crowning achievement, his African dioramas in the American Museum of Natural History, evoke awe even today, nearly a century after they were unveiled. He was, and remains, in a class by himself, the Michelangelo of his craft.

GROWING UP ON A FARM IN upstate New York, Carl Akeley knew at an early age what his calling would be. Although he cheerfully performed milking, haying, and other chores expected of any farm boy, it was in the surrounding woods and wetlands that he felt most at home. Under the guidance of a neighbor named Mitchell, young Carl learned to track and shoot and to hunt fox and raccoon behind Mitchell's pack of baying hounds. His interest in taxidermy began with visits to relatives in nearby Rochester, in whose homes he found stuffed versions of many of the same animals he hunted on the farm. But these deer heads and mounted birds were crude renderings of the splendid creatures he knew in the wild. Taxidermy was still in its infancy, and most mountings were little more than skins stuffed with cotton and sewn up with the stitches showing.

Even at age twelve, Akeley thought he could do better, and his first mounting — a neighbor's dead canary, which he perched in a lifelike pose on a twig — was an improvement over anything seen in the parlors of his city cousins. Guided by a mail-order book on taxidermy, he began filling his parents' house with skillfully arranged tableaux of quail, grouse, woodchuck, and other game collected on his hunting forays. By age sixteen he was passing out business cards reading "Carl E. Akeley — Artistic Taxidermy in All Its Branches."

In 1883, at age nineteen, Akeley left the farm to apprentice himself to Henry A. Ward, one of the leading taxidermists of his day, whose Rochester studio supplied mountings to museums all over the country. Even at Ward's, however, Akeley found the techniques to be rudimentary, requiring, as he later recalled, "little science and no art at all." Ward and his assistants possessed scant knowledge of the animals they mounted and stuffed them with rags and excelsior as if they were chairs or sofas. On his own, Akeley studied anatomy, memorizing the Latin names of bones and muscles, and he came up with new ways of skinning specimens that made it easier to hide the seams once the skins were sewn. Ward cast a skeptical eye on Akeley's perfectionism, for his brilliant apprentice worked slowly, and time was money. Moreover, the museums that were his main customers did not demand such realism. Yet it was Akeley to whom Ward entrusted the biggest job his studio ever attempted: the mounting of Jumbo, P.T. Barnum's famous elephant, after it was killed in a train wreck.

Having learned all he could from Ward, Akeley at age twenty-two moved on to the Milwaukee Public Museum and later to the new Field Museum, in Chicago. Over the next ten years he continued to experiment with new ways of mounting animals, always with the goal of exhibiting them as naturally as possible. A family of muskrats completed for the Milwaukee museum was his first habitat group, containing on a small scale the same elements that would later appear in his magnificent displays of African game. The diorama offered a cutaway view of a muskrat dome (a stick house similar to a beaver dam), showing the animals in activities above and below the water line.

A MORE AMBITIOUS PROJECT, for the Field Museum, consisted of four dioramas of a family of deer in spring, summer, fall, and winter. Akeley called it "The Four Seasons," and because of his obsession with detail, it took four years to complete. He developed techniques for creating artificial leaves — using colored beeswax, with fine wire and silk thread for the stems and veins — that made them indistinguishable from nature. Similar care went into the animals themselves, which Akeley collected on hunting trips to Northern Michigan. The body of each deer was first modeled in clay, with the leg bones and skull in place. From the clay model, he made a plaster cast that in turn served as the mold for a papier-mâché manikin on which the skin was mounted. Reinforced with wire mesh, the manikin weighed less than thirty pounds but was sturdy enough to support a man's weight; coated with shellac, it was impervious to moisture and could last indefinitely.

Akeley's move to the Field Museum enlarged his horizons. He and the museum's curator of zoology, Daniel Elliot, envisioned a major exhibition devoted to African wildlife, and in 1896 they sailed to East Africa to collect specimens. It was on this expedition, his first of five to Africa, that Akeley killed the leopard with his bare hands. Their tally also included cheetahs, wart hogs, spotted and striped hyenas, and many species of antelope, including a greater kudu, which Akeley killed at three hundred yards with a single shot to the head. (He regarded himself as only a fair marksman, so he was either lucky or overly modest.)

Following their return from Africa, Elliot and Akeley spent three months collecting North American animals in the Olympic Mountains of Washington State. Their take of 500 specimens included five Olympic elk and a mouse, new to science, that Elliot named *Peromyseus akeli* in his companion's honor.

In 1906, the Field Museum sent Akeley to Kenya and Uganda to expand its African collection. High up on the slopes of Mount Kenya he learned to stalk and shoot elephants under the guidance of the celebrated white hunter R.J. Cuninghame. Accompanying Akeley on the expedition was his wife, Delia (called Mickie), who was no mean shot herself. She and Carl each killed two elephants, and one of hers, a great bull, had the biggest tusks of any elephant ever shot on the mountain. Carl and Mickie had known each other since his days working for Henry Ward. Later, in Milwaukee and Chicago, she worked as his assistant. They married in 1902, when he was thirty-eight and she was twenty-seven.

Akeley made his third expedition to Africa in 1909. By then he had moved on to the American Museum of Natural History. Joining him on a day's hunt north of Lake Victoria was former president Theodore Roosevelt, in Akeley's view "the truest sportsman of them all," who had gone on an extended safari after leaving office. Several years before, Akeley had been a guest at the White House, and his stories about the big game of Africa had whetted T.R.'s resolve to hunt there. Akeley, Roosevelt, and the Roosevelt's twelve-year-old son, Kermit, enjoyed a productive day afield, each shooting an elephant; the three animals formed the nucleus of the museum's magnificent group of mounted elephants.

In many ways shooting an elephant was the easiest part of Akeley's job. The long process of skinning, preserving, and ultimately mounting the specimen now began. In the tropical heat it was critical to remove the skin as quickly as possible. After photographing and measuring the elephant, Akeley went to work with his skinning knife while his native assistants poured buckets of brine over the skin to keep it from spoiling. Removed in four large pieces, the skin weighed more than a ton and was two-and-a-half inches thick. Akeley put forty men to work flensing it for several days. The final layers of subcutaneous fat Akeley removed himself — a job that took another five days. Finally, the hides were salted, dried, and rolled in cloth soaked in beeswax.

The beeswax sealed the hides, protecting them until Akeley could prepare them for mounting. Once back at the museum, after softening the hides in a salt solution, he flensed them further, until they were only a quarter of an inch thick. The hides were then soaked in a tanning solution and rubbed with neats-foot oil until supple as a glove.

Now came the challenge of building a manikin and fitting the skin to it. The method Akeley evolved for mounting elephants used the skin itself as a kind of mold for the manikin. The mounting, which took Akeley and his two assistants several months, was done in three sections — right and left halves of the body, and the head. For each body section, Akeley began by building a frame of wire and cloth, over which he laid a thick coating of wet clay. The hide went on top of the clay. Like a masseur, Akeley worked the hide into the clay, kneading and shaping the materials into exactly the contours he wanted. Then he slathered a layer of plaster over the hide; once the plaster dried, it held the hide in place while he removed the underlying wire-cloth and clay. Next, he coated the inner surface of the hide with papier-mâché reinforced with wire netting. Dried and shellacked, the papier-mâché formed a permanent inner shell. After removing the outer plaster, Akeley and his assistants mounted the completed body sections onto a wooden frame. They fashioned the head in a similar manner and mounted it last, slipping it over a collar extending from the frame. Akeley sewed the skins together at the edges and covered up any exposed stitches with dyed beeswax.

He mounted an entire elephant herd this way. It is the stunning centerpiece of the American Museum of Natural History's African hall — a bull and several cows and juveniles, ears flaring and trunks extended in silent trumpeting at some unseen threat. In their naturalness and (often) dramatic tension, Akeley's mounts have the quality of world-class sculpture. He was, in fact, a sculptor of surpassing skill. His elephant group shares space with one of his finest works, a full-size bronze of Nandi spearmen attacking a pair of lions.

Akeley was also an accomplished inventor. He designed and patented a movie camera that recorded the motion of wild animals better than any before; it was used in World War I for aerial reconnaissance and later in Hollywood for filming action sequences. To create faux rock formations for his dioramas, he invented a compressed-air gun that sprayed stucco on wire mesh. It was adapted by the housing industry, and an industrial-scale version was made for spraying cement on bridges and other large structures.

The origins of the American Museum's African hall go back to an incident in 1910, toward the end of his third African expedition. He was hunting for elephants in the bamboo forests of Mount Kenya and had followed the footprints of an unusually large bull to a broad clearing. There, he found elephant droppings so fresh they were still steaming. The tracks led back into the forest. Akeley heard the crackling of bamboo and motioned his Kikuyu gun bearer to follow him. He had no sooner begun stalking the elephant when he sensed movement behind him and turned to see a huge gray mass bearing down on him. Before he could shoot, the elephant hit him like a battering ram. Akeley grabbed both tusks and swung between them as the elephant pressed him to the ground, its trunk hard against his chest. As he described the incident later, the last thing he remembered before blacking out was hearing a "wheezy grunt" and staring into the elephant's "wicked little eye."

He came to in a Nairobi hospital. The elephant had crushed his rib cage and ripped the skin off his face with its bristly trunk, but Akeley had survived. The elephant had driven its tusks deep into the soft earth, but they evidently hit a rock or root, stopping the forward thrust within an inch of Akeley's life.

Akeley had plenty of time to think during his six-month convalescence. He was forty-six now, and the elephant mauling gave him an appreciation for his own mortality. He reflected, too, on the primordial beauty of Africa and its astonishing wildlife. Since first coming there fifteen years before, he had seen the continent become gradually more civilized. Savanna and forest were giving way to farmland, and it was only a matter of time, he regretfully concluded, before the vast African herds went the way of the American bison. If the game itself couldn't be preserved, he could at least save some record of it. An idea took shape for a great hall of African mammals, with two galleries of forty dioramas encircling a centerpiece of mounted elephants.

The outbreak of World War I kept the project stalled in the planning stage, but in 1921 Akeley (now fifty-six) was able to return to Africa to collect specimens in the Kivu District of the Belgian Congo, near the border of what is now Zaire and Rwanda. Akeley's party included his adventurous twenty-three-year-old secretary, Martha Miller, the niece of a Chicago friend; his lawyer, Herbert Bradley; Bradley's wife, Mary; and the couple's five-year-old daughter and her nursemaid. Mary Hastings Bradley would go on to write *On the Gorilla Trail*, an engaging travelogue of their adventure.

Their destination, a spectacular region of cloud forests and volcanoes, was home to mountain gorillas living high on the slopes of Mount Mikeno. Akeley enjoyed hunting traditional game like elephant and kudu, but killing a creature so closely akin to humans was another matter. It took "all one's scientific ardour," he wrote, "to keep from feeling like a murderer." He would never forget the light fading from the eyes of a mortally wounded male and the "heartbreaking expression of piteous pleading on his face." Still, he relished the adventure of collecting in this exotic terrain. The first gorilla he shot tumbled down a slope, coming to rest in a tree overhanging a 300-foot chasm. Balanced on the branches, Akeley and his assistant skinned and skeletonized the gorilla on the spot, then hauled the skin and bones back up the slope with a rope.

The gorillas collected on this expedition became the group for what is arguably the greatest wildlife diorama ever created. It is certainly the most dramatic — a primordial scene of smoldering volcanoes and moss-festooned trees, dominated by a huge silverback male shot by Herbert Bradley. As usual, Akeley demanded absolute realism and spared no expense to achieve it. The vegetation alone, all of it artificial, would take six men an entire year to prepare. For a major diorama like the gorilla group Akeley budgeted $50,000, a figure that did not include the expense of acquiring the specimens. The cost today would be in the millions.

Following his return to the United States, Akeley championed the conservation of mountain gorillas. Thanks largely to his efforts, in 1925 the Belgian government established a national park to protect them.

Akeley made what would turn out to be his last safari in 1926. Financed by two of the museum's wealthiest patrons, Donald

Pomeroy and George Eastman (the latter of Eastman-Kodak fame), the expedition had the ambitious goal of collecting specimens for ten of the forty habitat groups proposed for the African hall. Akeley, by now divorced from Mickie, was accompanied by his second wife. Fourteen years younger than her husband, Mary Jobe Akeley was an explorer and adventurer in her own right, having led seven expeditions to the Canadian Rockies, one of whose peaks, Mount Jobe, is named in her honor. They had been married for just two years and regarded the Eastman-Pomeroy expedition as a kind of working honeymoon.

Carl Akeley was in his early sixties now, but he approached the expedition with the energy of a man half his age. Mary was astonished at her husband's ability to go all day on just four hours' sleep, and in the field he could walk everybody else into the ground. Most of the expedition was spent collecting specimens of plains animals, but Akeley also planned to revisit his beloved gorilla country. They were going back to Kivu to gather samples of vegetation needed to complete the gorilla diorama and to enable one of the expedition's artists, William Leigh, to do field sketches for the background panorama. Akeley had a strong personal reason for making the journey, too — the Edenic beauty of this unspoiled region haunted him, and he wanted to share it with Mary.

He spent the first six months of the expedition shooting in Tanganyika (today's Tanzania). Near the end of this period, he came down with malaria. His raging fever forced a return to Nairobi, but after a few weeks' convalescence, he appeared to have made a nearly complete recovery. Although still weak, he insisted on making the rough overland trip to Kivu according to schedule.

If Akeley pushed himself, he did so out of a growing sense of urgency about preserving his vision of Africa. Crossing southern Uganda, he despaired at the trackless wheat fields where, fifteen years before, he had hunted elephants with Teddy Roosevelt. In hundreds of miles they did not see a dozen animals — "Now it is desolation!" he told Mary. A Boer farmer who had settled in the region summed up the prevailing view: "All zebra must be shot. We must raise crops."

Kivu, at least, still represented the primitive Africa he had known, and despite a recurrence of fever, Akeley's spirits soared at the sight of it. Led by machete-wielding porters hacking a trail through the dense bamboo, the expedition ascended to his old camp, now almost completely overgrown.

The climb took several days and exhausted Akeley. Unable to shake his fever, he submitted to being carried part of the way in a hammock. By the time he reached the camp at 11,000 feet on the cold, misty saddle between mounts Mikeno and Karisimbi, he was racked by dysentery and unable to keep down food or drink. Over the next two days his condition grew worse. Although too weak to rise from his cot, Akeley remained lucid and seemed remarkably at peace. On the morning of the third day in camp, he began to hemorrhage internally. He died that afternoon.

Although Akeley didn't live to see the realization of his dream, the African hall was far enough along for him to die knowing it would be completed. He had wanted it named in honor of Theodore Roosevelt, but the museum's trustees had someone else in mind. The Akeley Hall of African Mammals officially opened May 19, 1936, on what would have been his seventy-second birthday.

No one considered returning Carl Akeley's body to civilization. "I want to die in the harness," he told Mary, "and I want to be buried in Africa." In twelve-hour shifts, two dozen porters worked three days excavating a grave in the lava rock of the slope overlooking his last camp, and he was laid to rest in the place he regarded as the most beautiful on Earth.

17

The Custer Wolf

It was said of the Custer Wolf that he could see an antelope blink and hear the wind ruffling a meadowlark's feathers a mile away. Certainly, in the fall of 1920, the ranchers of Custer County, South Dakota, whose livestock the wolf preyed on were convinced that he killed for sheer joy and delighted in mutilating his victims — tearing hunks of flesh from bawling cattle, bobtailing or castrating them with a single savage snap of his powerful jaws. In one week the previous spring he had killed thirty head and eaten only a portion of a few carcasses. Often when he did choose to feed, he showed what could only be seen as a ghoulish preference for unborn calves ripped from the womb.

Adding to the Custer Wolf's mystique was his white color and loner ways. Mateless, he ranged his territory between the Black Hills and Dakota Badlands with a pair of coyotes patrolling like bodyguards on his flanks.

In more than a decade of tracking wolves, the hunter Harry Williams had never encountered one that evoked such awe and fear or that had managed to beat the odds for so long. In a six-year reign of terror the Custer Wolf had destroyed an estimated $25,000 worth of livestock, a record few other renegades came close to matching. The $500 price on his head — ten times the normal wolf bounty — attracted legions of freelance trappers as well as sportsmen with packs of wolfhounds. The Custer Wolf evaded them all.

A legendary predator of livestock on the Dakota range, the Custer Wolf for years evaded the efforts of government hunters to trap and kill him.

Williams was a government hunter who by law could collect no bounty on any predatory animal. Anyway, it wasn't money but his reputation as Uncle Sam's best "wolfer" that kept him chasing the Custer Wolf. But after seven long months of fruitless pursuit he was almost ready to believe the clearly preposterous tales about the animal. *Ain't no normal wolf at all,* the ranchers swore. *He's half wolf and half mountain lion, as big as a pony. Some think he's gonna live forever. Bullets won't touch him, and you can forget traps or poison, too — he won't come near 'em.*

From our twenty-first-century perspective it can be hard to understand (and easy to condemn) the ranchers' hatred of wolves and predators generally and their single-minded determination to exterminate every last one. The reasons were both economic — predators killed livestock, after all — and cultural. They had inherited a centuries-old view of predators as wicked killers of the "good" animals, domestic and wild, on which humans depended for food and sport. The wolf drew special attention as a top predator and also as a symbol. Ranchers lived in a merciless environment that could wipe them out in any number of ways — blizzards, droughts, and prairie fires all took their toll; in his wildness and in the randomness of his attacks, the wolf embodied the capricious fury of that environment like no other animal.

Although we can only speculate about Williams's actual attitudes (the historical record tells us almost nothing about him) he was part of the ranchers' culture and must have shared their views, at least in part. But as a man who spent his life tracking wolves, he could also appreciate and admire their keen intelligence, even in the perverted form it sometimes took. Perhaps he even recognized that the vicious behavior of the Custer Wolf and similar renegades — their habits of mutilating and killing without eating — was an aberration, the product of the unnatural and highly stressed environment in which they operated.

As he got ready to set still another trap on this cool October evening, Williams may have sensed that the Custer Wolf's years of killing might soon be over. Perhaps he even felt a curious ambivalence about this prospect, for the empathy between hunter and prey had grown strong. However grudgingly, Williams respected the Custer Wolf and marveled at the animal's ability to elude him.

In his mind he replayed their long game of hide and seek. He remembered his first glimpse of the wolf loping with his coyote escort. Williams shot the coyotes — a calculated risk that would put the wolf on his guard, although he had to get the coyotes out of the way if he were ever going to get a shot at the wolf himself. The gambit backfired, for the wolf became extremely wary and never exposed himself to Williams again. Wherever possible he took to streambeds, outcrops, or fallen timber to avoid leaving tracks. Several times he made kills, then wandered from them and doubled back on his own trail to spy on the hunter. Williams had known bears to do this but never wolves.

Luck also ran with the Custer Wolf, for more than once Williams had come within a hare's breath of bagging him, only to have him slip from his grasp. In early August the wolf had reappeared in the territory following a month's absence, killing and gorging on several steers. Williams picked up his trail and followed it to the mouth of a canyon. He knew the wolf would be sleeping off his dinner and with a careful stalk would be easy picking. He tethered his horse and was just entering the canyon on foot when two riders galloped up shouting news of another wolf kill. Williams tried to hush them, but the riders came on like a stampede, waking the wolf and allowing him to escape.

Despite the Custer Wolf's alleged aversion to them, Williams had succeeded five times in luring him into traps he had set. The first two times the wolf stepped on the jaws of the trap without springing it. The third time he rolled on the trap, setting it off but escaping with the loss of a few tufts of hair. The last two incidents were even more frustrating, and Williams couldn't think about them without shaking his head in disbelief: twice the wolf sprung the trap and was caught, yet both times managed to pull his foot free.

The wolf was damn lucky, all right, and maybe a damn fool too. In the last few months he had showed incredible bravado, passing up range stock to raid barnyards and stock pens at the very doorsteps of his enemy, slashing through horses, sheep, cows, and farms dogs. Roused by the animals' terrified noises, ranchers leapt from their beds and grabbed their guns. But the wolf killed with astonishing quickness, and the closest anyone came to him was a glimpse of his ghostly form slipping out of range in the moonlight.

In the last six years hundreds of men had done everything they could to get the Custer Wolf and all had failed. But the relentless pursuit had taken its toll on the old renegade. Maybe he was tired of the game and took more chances because he wanted it over. Williams liked to think so, anyway. He didn't know how many traps he had prepared for the Custer Wolf but hoped this one would be the last.

As a professional wolf hunter, he had gone through the ritual thousands of times. The first step was identifying the wolf's runway or hunting route, which even the Custer Wolf, for all his unpredictability, tended to follow with lupine regularity. The runway ran the perimeter of the wolf's territory and was marked by scent posts — bushes, rocks, or bunch grass where the wolf urinated. A trained eye could spot one of these posts by the wolf's ground scratchings, and it was here that the wolfer set his trap.

Before approaching the site he did everything possible to rid himself and his equipment of human smell. Boots, gloves, trap, ground cloth, and a short wooden shovel were cured in a manure pile for a week or more beforehand. The wolfer kneeled on the cloth and used it for piling dirt excavated from the shallow, flat-bottomed hole he dug for the trap. Attached to the trap was a length of chain connected to a steel stake. With his shovel, he hammered the stake into the hole until it was flush with the bottom, then set the trap and laid it carefully in the hole. After placing a piece of window screen over the trap pan (or trigger), he backfilled the hole. The site was smoothed over and any leftover dirt removed.

To lure his prey the wolfer concocted an aromatic gruel. A government pamphlet gave the following recipe: "Put into a bottle the urine from a wolf, the gall, and the anal glands, which are situated under the skin on either side of the vent and resemble small pieces of bluish fat … . In preparing 4 ounces of the mixture use one-quarter the amount of glycerin to give it body and prevent too rapid evaporation, and 1 grain of corrosive sublimate to keep it from spoiling. Let the mixture stand several days, then shake well before using."

Sometimes wolfers raised orphaned pups as a source for these grisly ingredients, but usually they were saved from the carcasses of wolves they had trapped or shot. Williams recalled the Custer Wolf's excitement when he came across the scent he had prepared from a she-wolf's glands. To his amazement, the wolf reacted by returning to a remote part of his territory and preparing several old dens — the aging bachelor thought he had found a mate. In fact, the Custer Wolf was a widower, having lost his only mate in a trap four years before; it was part of the lore surrounding him that he had spent the rest of his life avenging her death.

For this trap Williams had a special batch of scent, made earlier in the year and held in reserve for just such an occasion. He followed the same recipe but used parts exclusively from a notorious stock killer he had trapped the previous winter near Split Rock, Wyoming. The Split Rock Wolf destroyed $10,000 worth of livestock, and, like the Custer Wolf, had dodged his pursuers for years before Williams abruptly ended his career. Of course, Williams knew there was no reason why a scent from this particular wolf would work better than one from any other, but he would play his hunch anyway. He uncorked the bottle and sprinkled the contents around the trap. Now there was nothing left to do but return to camp and wait.

The fear and hatred directed at the Custer Wolf was part of a long if not especially honorable tradition. The ancient Greeks were the first to place bounties on wolves, while legends of werewolves and grotesque fairy tales like Little Red Riding Hood bespeak of the deep loathing they evoked among Williams's European ancestors. In the New World, the Massachusetts and Virginia colonies had wolf bounties on their statutes by the 1630s, and Pennsylvania employed professional wolf hunters throughout most of the eighteenth century.

As Americans moved west and settled their vast continent, they waged an unrelenting pogrom against the wolf. The tools of extirpation included wooden and steel traps, rifles and set guns, pens and pits and snares. But the most efficient weapon was strychnine, a poison derived from a plant known by a variety of common names: Quaker button, poison nut, vomiting bean. Strychnine attacked the central nervous system, bringing on convulsions and death. It was cheap and abundant and easily transportable in crystal form. On the prairies following the Civil War, wolfers mixed the crystals with water for lacing buffalo carcasses. A single carcass might kill a dozen wolves.

Wolves were easy game for anyone armed with strychnine, and by the twentieth century only remnant populations could be found throughout the West. With buffalo and most other wild game gone, the remaining wolves turned inevitably to the domestic herds that had replaced them. The ranchers who kept these herds had about as much use for wolves and other predators as they did for the Indians now confined to reservations. Indians and wolves were part of the same hostile country the ranchers were determined to conquer, and nothing in their eyes could be more alien than the Indian's respectful view of the wolf as a symbol of stealth and courage. The Custer Wolf's territory included the Sioux reservation at Pine Ridge, where aging veterans of the Little Big Horn must have smiled at his depredations against the white ranchers.

The West's remaining wolves adapted to the new environment. A few even thrived in it. Only the very smartest could survive the white man's ruthless war of extermination, and the winnowing led to a kind of Darwinian selection that placed an absolute premium on cunning. A new superbreed of wolf — wiser, tougher, and warier than any before — seemed to result. Many of this breed became infamous destroyers of stock, their colorful monikers — the Unaweep Wolf, Big Foot, Three Toes, Traveler, Rags the Digger, the Fruita Phantom, Old Guy Jumbo, and most infamous of all, the Custer Wolf — engraved in Western lore as surely as the names of Crazy Horse and Geronimo.

Not surprisingly, ranchers refused to put up with continuing raids on their stock, and with help from the U.S. Biological Survey (the forerunner of today's Fish & Wildlife Service) launched an all-out campaign against wolves and other predators. The government hired more than three hundred professional hunters (Williams among them) and appropriated hundreds of thousands of dollars for the program. Between

1915 and 1920, their efforts accounted for a staggering total of wildlife that included 110,000 coyotes, 15,000 bobcats and lynxes, and 3,000 wolves. Only animals shot or trapped were counted; estimates of those killed by strychnine bring the total to 250,000, a figure that still doesn't include the "incidental" poisoning of such nontarget animals as skunks and other small mammals and birds of prey.

The Custer Wolf survived this furious assault to become, by this cold October night in 1920, the Biological Survey's unofficial Public Enemy Number One. The sky in the east was just beginning to brighten as the wolf left the rock ledge where he had spent the night. He soon picked up the scent of another wolf. It was different from the other wolf scents he had noticed along his runway in the last few months — scents that, after three terrifying escapes, he now firmly associated with traps. Torn between fear and curiosity, he circled the familiar scent post. Part of him wanted to flee, but the part that told him to erase the interloper's scent with his own won out. Nose to the ground, he inched closer. All his senses were alert for the slightest thing wrong — a blade of grass or pebble out of place, or the faintest human smell. He paused, sniffed, and took another step. For a split second the ground's unnatural softness registered on his brain before the dirt exploded and the steel jaws closed on his foot.

At his campsite several miles away, Williams rose before dawn and walked to where he had set the trap the previous day. He was not surprised to find his old adversary waiting for him. The wolf sat resting on the ground, head raised and eyes alert, panting. At the sight of Williams he leapt so hard that the stake holding the trap pulled free. Wolf, trap, chain, and stake took off, but Williams knew the wolf could not get far and followed at a leisurely pace. In his official report he laconically described the end of the Custer Wolf:

> He stepped into a trap in the morning and it got a good grip on him. He ran with it about one hundred fifty yards when the hook caught

> on a tree, but that did not seem to stop him at all. He broke the swivel of the trap and ran on with it on his front foot. I trailed him three miles and got a shot at him and got him. He has been so lucky that I expected the gun would fail to shoot, but it worked O.K.

Williams was struck by the animal's size. From ranchers' accounts he had expected a monster, yet this feared killer was "smaller than the average male wolf," weighing ninety-eight pounds and measuring six feet from nose to tail. "His teeth would be good for fifteen years longer. He broke some of them off on the trap but aside from that they were in good condition. He is an old wolf with a fur that is almost white."

The government's anti-predator campaign didn't end with the Custer Wolf's death but continued, albeit with less intensity, for years to come. Gradually, attitudes changed as conservationists like Aldo Leopold argued for a new wildlife ethos that recognized predators as essential elements in a healthy ecosystem. In a famous passage from "Thinking like a Mountain," a chapter in his conservation classic, *A Sand County Almanac*, Leopold described an epiphany he had as a young man in Arizona after he and some friends killed a she-wolf and her cubs:

> We reached the old wolf in time to watch a fierce green fire dying in her eyes. I realized then, and have known ever since, that there was something new to me in those eyes — something known only to her and to the mountain. I was young then, and full of trigger-itch; I thought that because fewer wolves meant more deer, that no wolves would mean a hunter's paradise. But after seeing the green fire die, I sensed that neither the wolf nor the mountain agreed with such a view.

The new ethos would come too late for the gray wolf, which alone among major predators was completely extirpated from the American West. They survived north of the border, however. In the 1980s, a few wolves wandered into Glacier National Park from Canada, and they were later successfully reintroduced into Yellowstone National Park. In 2009 the federal government removed them from the Endangered Species List.

Instead of skinning the Custer Wolf on the spot, Williams took the carcass to a nearby ranch and propped it on a stick for photographs. In one picture, Williams holds a carbine and stands straight-on toward the camera. He is tall and lean, and his handsome face looks intelligent and surprisingly young. The ranch owner, an older man in a three-piece suit and fedora, rests an arm on the hunter's shoulder, sharing in his triumph. The Custer Wolf stands at their feet, legs splayed and head held low as if in submission, a pose he would never have struck in life.

NOTES, SOURCES, ACKNOWLEDGMENTS

The seventeen pieces in *The Last Buffalo Hunt and Other Stories of the Great American Outdoors* were first published in magazine form between 1978 and 2001. Thirteen of them were written for *Field & Stream*, three for *American West*, and one (about the naturalist William Bartram) for the British magazine *History Today*. As noted below, all of them here have been adapted, sometimes extensively, from the originals.

I am indebted to Duncan Barnes and to other editors at *Field & Stream*, including Slaton White, Dave Petzal, Lynne Peel, and the late Maggie Nichols. Also to *F&S* columnists George Reiger and the late Gene Hill, and to publisher Francis Pandolfi.

—J.I.M.

1. Daniel Boone: The Long Hunter

Adapted from "Daniel Boone" (one in a series of articles on "Great American Hunters"), *Field & Stream*, December 2001.

Draper, Lyman C. *The Life of Daniel Boone*. Mechanicsburg, Pa.: Stackpole Books, 1998.

Faragher, John Mack. *Daniel Boone: The Life and Legend of an American Pioneer.* New York: Henry Holt, 1992. 2.

2. William Bartram in America's Eden

Adapted from "William Bartram in America's Eden," *History Today*, November 1978.

Earnest, Ernest. *John and William Bartram: Botanists and Explorers.* Philadelphia: University of Pennsylvania Press, 1940.

Harper, Francis, ed. *The Travels of William Bartram.* Athens: University of Georgia Press, 1998.

3. George Drouillard: Lewis & Clark's Indispensable Man

Adapted from "'This Excellent Hunter,'" *Field & Stream,* June 1992.

Holmberg, James J. "A Man of Much Merit." *We Proceeded On* (journal of the Lewis and Clark Trail Heritage Foundation), August 2000.

Moulton, Gary E., ed. *The Journals of the Lewis and Clark Expedition*, 13 volumes. Lincoln: University of Nebraska Press, 1983-2001.

Sandoz, Mari. *The Beaver Men: Spearheads of Empire.* Lincoln: University of Nebraska Press, 1964.

Skarsten, M.O. *George Drouillard: Hunter and Interpreter for Lewis and Clark and Fur Trader, 1807-1810.* Spokane, Wash.: Arthur H. Clark, 2003.

Walcheck, Kenneth C. "'We eat an emensity of meat.'" *We Proceeded On*, August 2006.

4. Going Native

Adapted from "White Indians," *Field & Stream,* August 1992.

Axtell, James. *The European and the Indian: Essays in the Ethnohistory of Colonial North America.* New York: Oxford University Press, 1981.

Drake, Samuel G. *Life in the Wigwam.* Buffalo, N.Y.: Derby, Orton and Mulligan, 1853.

Drinnon, Richard. *White Savage: The Case of John Dunn Hunter.* New York: Schocken Books, 1972.

Hunter, John D. *Memoirs of a Captivity among the Indians of North America.* New York: Schocken Books, 1973.

Tanner, John. *The Falcon: A Narrative of the Captivity and Adventures of John Tanner.* New York: Penguin Group, Penguin Nature Classics, 1994.

VanDerBeets, Richard. *The Indian Captivity Narrative: An American Genre.* Lanham, Md.: University Press of America, 1984.

5. The Right Stuff: Mountain Men and Voyageurs

Adapted from "The Right Stuff," *Field & Stream,* November 1994.

Clyman, James. *Journal of a Mountain Man.* Missoula: Mountain Press Publishing Co., 1984.

DeVoto, Bernard. *Across the Wide Missouri.* Boston: Houghton Mifflin Co., 1947.

Hafen, LeRoy R., ed. *Ruxton of the Rockies.* Norman: University of Oklahoma Press, 1950.

Gilbert, Bil. *Westering Man: The Life of Joseph Walker, Master of the Frontier.* New York: Atheneum, 1983.

Morgan, Dale L. *Jedediah Smith and the Opening of the West.* Lincoln: University of Nebraska Press, Bison Books, 1964.

Russell, Osborne. *Journal of a Trapper.* Lincoln: University of Nebraska Press, Bison Books, 1965.

Ruxton, George Frederick Ruxton. *Life in the Far West.* Norman: University of Oklahoma Press, 1951.

Townsend, John Kirk. *Narrative of a Journey Across the Rocky Mountains to the Columbia River.* Lincoln: University of Nebraska Press, 1978.

Utley, Robert M. *A Life Wild and Perilous: Mountain Men and the Paths to the Pacific.* New York: Henry Holt, 1997.

Weber, David J. *The Taos Trappers: The Fur Trade in the Far Southwest, 1540-1846.* Norman: University of Oklahoma Press, 1968.

6. Frank Forester: The Exile

Adapted from "The Exile," *Field & Stream*, December 1996.

Beverly-Giddings, A.R. *Frank Forester on Upland Shooting.* New York: William Morrow, 1951.

Herbert, Henry William [Frank Forester]. *Sporting Scenes and Characters.* Philadelphia: T.B. Peterson, 1881.

Hunt, William S. *Frank Forester, a Tragedy in Exile.* Newark, N.J.: Carteret Book Co., 1933.

Reiger, George. *Profiles in Saltwater Angling.* Englewood Cliffs, N.J.: Prentice Hall, 1973.

Reiger, John F. *American Sportsmen and the Origins of Conservation.* Corvallis: Oregon State University Press, 2001.

7. John Muir in the Sierra

Adapted from "Turning Point: John Muir in the Sierra, 1871," *American West,* July-August 1979.

Bade, W.F., ed. *The Life and Letters of John Muir,* Vol. 1. Boston: Houghton Mifflin, 1924.

Farquhar, Francis P. *History of the Sierra Nevada.* Berkeley: University of California Press, 1965.

Fox, Stephen. *John Muir and His Legacy: The American Conservation Movement.* Boston: Little, Brown, 1981.

Merrill, George P. *The First One Hundred Years of American Geology.* New Haven: Yale University Press, 1924.

Muir, John. "Living Glaciers of California." *Overland Monthly,* December 1972.

Thayer, James B. *A Western Journey with Mr. Emerson.* Boston: Little, Brown, 1884.

Wolfe, Linnie Marsh. *Son of the Wilderness: The Life of John Muir.* New York: Alfred A. Knopf, 1945.

8. King of Diamonds

Adapted from "Clarence King, Adventurous Geologist," *American West,* July-August 1982.

Harpending, Asbury. *The Great Diamond Hoax.* Norman: University of Oklahoma Press, 1958.

King, Clarence. *Mountaineering in the Sierra Nevada.* Lincoln: University of Nebraska Press, 1970.

Sandweiss, Martha A. *Passing Strange: A Gilded Age Tale of Love and Deception Across the Color Line.* New York: Penguin Press, 2009.

Wilkins, Thurman. *Clarence King: A Biography.* New York: Macmillan, 1958.

Wilson, Robert. "The Great Diamond Hoax of 1872." *Smithsonian,* June 2004.

9. William Henry Jackson: Photographing the Frontier

Adapted from "William Henry Jackson," *American West*, September/October 1980.

Findley, Rowe. "The Life and Times of William Henry Jackson." *National Geographic*, February 1989.

Hafen, LeRoy R. and Ann W., eds. *The Diaries of William Henry Jackson.* Glendale, Calif.: A.H. Clarke, 1959.

Jackson, Clarence S. *Picture Maker of the Old West.* New York: Charles Scribner's Sons, 1947.

________. *Pageant of the Pioneers.* Minden, Nev.: H. Warp Pioneer Village, 1958.

Jackson, William Henry. *Time Exposure.* New York: G.P. Putnam's, 1940.

Jackson, William Henry, and Driggs, Howard R. *The Pioneer Photographer: Rocky Mountain Adventures with a Camera.* Yonkers-on-Hudson: World Book Co., 1929.

10. Custer Goes Hunting

Adapted from "Custer Goes Hunting," *Field & Stream*, July 1999.

Ambrose, Steven E. *Crazy Horse and Custer.* New York: Doubleday, 1975.

Barnett, Louise. *Touched by Fire: The Life, Death, and Mythic Afterlife of George Armstrong Custer.* New York: Henry Holt, 1996.

Bourke, John G. *On the Border with Crook.* Lincoln: University of Nebraska Press, Bison Books, 1971.

Connell, Evan S. *Son of the Morning Star: Custer and the Little Big Horn.* San Francisco: North Point Press, 1984.

Custer, Elizabeth B. *Boots and Saddles.* Bowie, Md.: Heritage Books, 1990.

————. *Following the Guidon.* Norman: University of Oklahoma Press, 1966.

———. *Tenting on the Plains.* New York: C.L. Webster, 1887.

Custer, George A. *My Life on the Plains.* Norman: University of Oklahoma Press, 1976.

Dippie, Brian W., ed. *Nomad: George A. Custer in Turf, Field and Farm.* Austin: University of Texas Press, 1980.

Grinnell, George Bird. *Two Great Scouts and Their Pawnee Guides.* Lincoln: University of Nebraska Press, Bison Books, 1973.

Millbrook, Minnie Dubbs. "Big Game Hunting with the Custers, 1869-1870." *Kansas Historical Quarterly,* Winter 1975.

Sprague, Marshall. *A Gallery of Dudes.* Boston: Little, Brown, 1967.

Utley, Robert M. *Cavalier in Buckskin: Custer and the Western Military Frontier.* Norman: University of Oklahoma Press, 1988.

11. THE LAST BUFFALO HUNT

Adapted from "The Last Buffalo Hunt," *Field & Stream,* February 1986. A version of this article was also anthologized in *The Best of Field & Stream: 100 Years of Great Writing from America's Premier Sporting Magazine* (Lyons & Burford, 1995).

Adams, Alexander B. *Sitting Bull: An Epic of the Plains.* N.Y.: Putnam Sons, 1973.

Branch, E. Douglas. *The Hunting of the Buffalo.* Lincoln: University of Nebraska Press, Bison Books, 1962.

Brown, Dee. *Bury My Heart at Wounded Knee: An Indian History of the American West.* Holt, Rinehart and Winston, 1971.

Burdick, Usher L. *Tales from Buffalo Land.* Baltimore: Wirth Brothers, 1939.

Dary, David A. *The Buffalo Book: The Full Saga of the American Animal.* Chicago: The Swallow Press, 1974.

Garretson, Martin A. *A Short History of the American Bison.* Freeport, N.Y.: Books for Libraries Press, 1971.

Hornaday, William T. *The Extermination of the American Bison.*

Washington, D.C.: Smithsonian Institution Press, 2002. (First published as part of Smithonian annual report for 1887.)

McLaughlin, James. *My Friend the Indian.* Boston: Houghton Mifflin Co., 1910.

Mitchell, John G. "Saved just in time, the buffalo graze again on the plains." *Smithsonian,* May 1981.

Rorabacher, J. Albert. *The American Buffalo in Transition.* St. Cloud, Minn.: North Star Press, 1970.

Russell, Franklin. *The Hunting Animal.* N.Y.: Harper & Row, 1983.

Sandoz, Mari. *The Buffalo Hunters.* New York: Hastings House, 1954.

Utley, Robert M. *The Last Days of the Sioux Nation.* New Haven: Yale University Press, 1963.

12. Out West with T.R.

Adapted from "Theodore Roosevelt — Western Sportsman," *Field & Stream,* September 1990.

McCullough, David. *Mornings on Horseback.* New York: Simon & Schuster, 1981.

Morris, Edmund. *The Rise of Theodore Roosevelt.* New York: Coward, McCann and Geoghegan, 1979.

Roosevelt, Theodore. *Hunting Trips of a Ranchman.* New York: G.P. Putnam's Sons, 1886.

13. Planting Fish and Playing God

Adapted from "Planting Fish and Playing God," *Field & Stream,* June 1997.

Behnke, Robert. "Livingston Stone, J.B. Campbell, and the Origins of Hatchery Rainbow Trout." *The American Fly Fisher,* Fall 1990.

Green, Seth. *Trout Culture.* Caledonia, N.Y.: Curtis, Morey, 1870.

Mather, Fred. *Modern Fishculture in Fresh and Salt Water.* New York: Forest and Stream Publishing, 1900.

————. *My Angling Friends.* New York: Forest and Stream Publishing, 1901.

Merritt, J.I. "Hunting Dr. Slack: American Fish Culture's Forgotten Man." *The American Fly Fisher*, Winter 2011.

Norris, J. Robert. "Visiting with Uncle Thad: Thaddeus Norris, 1811-1877." *The American Fly Fisher*, Winter 1995.

Norris, Thaddeus. *American Fish Culture.* Philadelphia: Porter & Coates, 1898.

Stone, Livingston. *Domesticated Trout.* Boston: James R. Osgood, 1872.

14. Call Me Nessmuk

Adapted from "Wild Man Nessmuk," *Field & Stream*, February 1998.

Brenan, Dan, ed. *Canoeing the Adirondacks with Nessmuk: The Adirondack Letters of George Washington Sears.* Mountain Lake, N.Y.: The Adirondack Museum/Syracuse University Press, 1993.

Jerome, Christine. *An Adirondack Passage: The Cruise of the Canoe Sairy Gamp.* New York: HarperCollins, 1994.

Lyon, Robert. "The Odyssey of Nessmuk." *The Conservationist* (journal of the N.Y. Department of Environmental Conservation), March-April 1992.

Mather, Fred. *My Angling Friends.* New York: Forest and Stream Publishing, 1901.

Sears, George Washington [Nessmuk]. *Woodcraft and Camping.* New York: Dover Publications, 1963.

Verner, William. "Nessmuk and the Cruise of the Sairy Gamp." *The Conservationist*, May-June 1976.

15. Ishi: America's Last Wild Indian

Adapted from "The Heritage of the Bow," *Field & Stream*, January 1988.

Kroeber, Theodora. *Ishi in Two Worlds: A Biography of the Last Wild Indian in North America.* Berkeley: University of California Press, 1961.

Pope, Saxton. "Archery Ancient and Modern." *Field & Stream*, January 1925.

16. Carl Akeley: Michelangelo of Taxidermy

Adapted from "Carl Akeley, the Man Who Loved Africa," *Field & Stream*, January 1991. With its emphasis on Africa, this piece is something of an outlier for a book about the American outdoors. But Akeley seems to me an essentially American type, and I am partial to him for personal reasons: my paternal grandmother's first cousin, Martha Miller Bliven, whom I knew as a child as "Aunt" Martha, was a member of Akeley's 1921 gorilla expedition.

Akeley, Carl E. *In Brightest Africa.* Garden City, N.Y.: Garden City Publishing, 1927.

Akeley, Mary L. Jobe. *The Wilderness Lives Again: Carl Akeley and the Great Adventure.* New York: Dodd, Mead, 1940.

Bodry-Sanders, Penelope. *Carl Akeley: Africa's Collector, Africa's Savior.* New York: Paragon House, 1991.

Bradley, Mary Hasting. *On the Gorilla Trail.* Mechanicsburg, Pa.: Stackpole Books, 2005 (originally published in 1922 by Appleton).

Kirk, Jay. *Kingdom Under Glass.* New York: Henry Holt, 2010.

Preston, Douglas J. *Dinosaurs in the Attic: An Excursion into the American Museum of Natural History.* New York: St. Martin's, 1986.

17. The Custer Wolf

Adapted from "The Custer wolf," *Field & Stream*, March 1988. The article misidentified the hunter as "R.P." Williams. His initials were "H.P." and he went by the name Harry, according to personal correspondence from a reader, Harry Babcock of Long Pine, Nebraska, who remembered Williams from his boyhood on a ranch in Wyoming.

Bell, W.B. "Hunting Down Stock Killers." *Yearbook of the Department of Agriculture*, 1920. Washington, D.C.: Government Printing Office, 1920.

Caras, Roger A. *The Custer Wolf: Biography of an American Ren-*

egade. Boston: Little, Brown, 1966.

Leopold, Aldo. *A Sand County Almanac.* New York: Oxford University Press, 1949.

"Trapping on the Farm." *Yearbook of the Department of Agriculture, 1919.* Washington, D.C.: Government Printing Office, 1919.

Young, Stanley P. *The Last of the Loners.* New York: Macmillan, 1970.

Young, Stanley P. and Edward A. Goldman. *The Wolves of North America.* Washington, D.C.: American Wildlife Institute, 1944.

Index

Index

About the Author

J.I. (John I., "Jim") Merritt is the author of *Baronets and Buffalo: The British Sportsman in the American West, 1833-1881* (Mountain Press Publishing, 1985), *Goodbye, Liberty Belle: A Son's Search for His Father's War* (Wright State University Press, 1993, and Cooper Square Press, 2002), and *Trout Dreams: A Gallery of Fly-Fishing Profiles* (Derrydale Press, 2000). He has also compiled and edited three anthologies: *The Best of Field & Stream: 100 Years of Great Writing from America's Premier Sporting Magazine* (Lyons & Burford, 1995), *The Best of PAW: 100 Years of the Princeton Alumni Weekly* (Princeton Alumni Publications, 2000), and *The Derrydale Press Treasury of Fishing* (The Derrydale Press, 2002). For many years he was a contributing editor at *Field & Stream.* Merritt is a former editor of Princeton University's alumni magazine (1989-99) and *We Proceeded On*, the quarterly journal of the Lewis and Clark Trail Heritage Foundation (2000-06). He has written nearly two hundred magazine articles on fishing and the outdoors, the American West, natural history, science, and other subjects. He and his wife, Nancy, live in Pennington, New Jersey.

This book was typeset in
12-point Adobe Caslon.
Design and layout by the author.
Printed on acid-free paper.